How to Do It NOW

Because It's *Not* Going Away

How to Do It NOW

Because It's *Not* Going Away

An Expert Guide to Getting Stuff Done

LESLIE JOSEL

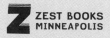

ZEST BOOKS
MINNEAPOLIS

For my husband, Wayne, my true partner in every way.

To my perfectly imperfect kids, Maddie and Eli, whom I aspire to be more like when I grow up.

And a special dedication to my students, so your stories can be shared and your voices heard.

Zest Books™
An imprint of Lerner Publishing Group, Inc.
241 First Avenue North
Minneapolis, MN 55401 USA

For reading levels and more information, look up this title at www.lernerbooks.com.

Visit us at zestbooks.net.

Design by Mary Ross
Main body text set in Century Schoolbook Std.
Typeface provided by Monotype Typography.

Library of Congress Cataloging-in-Publication Data

Names: Josel, Leslie, author.
Title: How to do it now because it's not going away : an expert guide to getting stuff done / Leslie Josel.
Description: Minneapolis : Zest Books, [2020] | Includes index. | Audience: Ages 13–18 | Audience: Grades 7–9 | Summary: "Packed with practical solutions and tips to stay on top of homework, develop a sense of time, manage digital distractions, and create easy-to-follow routines, this guide will help teens stop procrastinating and get their tasks done"— Provided by publisher.
Identifiers: LCCN 2020001477 (print) | LCCN 2020001478 (ebook) | ISBN 9781541581579 (library binding) | ISBN 9781541581616 (paperback) | ISBN 9781728401621 (ebook)
Subjects: LCSH: Students—Time management—Juvenile literature. | Study skills—Juvenile literature.
Classification: LCC LB3607.8 .J67 2020 (print) | LCC LB3607.8 (ebook) | DDC 371.30281—dc23

LC record available at https://lccn.loc.gov/2020001477
LC ebook record available at https://lccn.loc.gov/2020001478

Manufactured in the United States of America
1-47341-47967-4/21/2020

CONTENTS

If you're reading this book, I'm thinking it's because someone else might have suggested it to you. Why do I think that? Because every day, five times a day, as an academic/life coach for teens, I'm speaking to parents about their concerns regarding your procrastination. And these discussions are fraught with emotion, anxiety and confusion. So if I'm having these conversations with your parents, I'm assuming you are too.

My goal in writing this book is to help you understand why you procrastinate, and provide support, guidance and real advice so you can develop and implement strategies to manage it.

And in doing so, I've included A LOT of information. So before you dive in, I want to remind you of a few things: The book is meant as a guide, one to pick up again and again, whether to learn a new set of skills or just as a refresher. Some of the strategies will hit home immediately, and others you will dismiss outright. Some of the methods are meant for high schoolers, others for college students. To get the most out of this book, go through it at your own pace, on your own time and in your own way.

Just to be clear, the book isn't preachy or bossy or filled with endless statistics and research that you won't read or care much about. I offer no judgment or absolutes. No one-size-fits-all solutions. Just straight-up, user-friendly tips.

So now that I've given you some pointers for how to get the most out of this book, here's what I DON'T want you to do:

1. **DON'T stress out.** Since I've written a book with tons of strategies and suggestions, some of you will feel as if you have to do all of them . . . at the same time. That could not be further from the truth.

The goal here is NOT to have you do everything at once, think you are not doing enough or, worse, doing everything wrong.

2. **DON'T try to absorb everything at once and immediately implement every single strategy discussed here.** After reading through the book (or going back to peruse the table of contents), start with one area or aspect of your life that you'd most like to work on and focus on implementing the tools in that chapter. Remember, the goal is to try a little at a time and keep it manageable.

3. **DON'T think these solutions are intended as a quick fix.** This process takes effort and patience. If you see that a tool is working, great! And if it's not, no worries. Move on. If all you do is develop one specific strategy that helps you manage your procrastination, you should consider that a victory since that one, newly developed skill could make all the difference in the world and will most likely facilitate the learning of another.

4. **DON'T think you need to be on a schedule.** When it comes to developing skills to manage your procrastination tendencies, there is no clock or calendar. I can't tell you how long it will be until you see progress. For some, a particular strategy may bring fast results. For others, it may take months before you will effectively use one of these techniques. There are simply too many variables at play. But as I've seen in my work, you tend to have an innate sense of whether something will work and how long it will take for you to grab on.

Don't get discouraged. Trust yourself. Keep working at it and try different approaches until you find what does work. Go slow. Keep throwing things against the wall and see what sticks. Developing the skills necessary to manage procrastination is truly a work in progress. Let's get started.

Visit howtodoitnowbook.com to download the forms and charts you'll find in this book, as well as other useful tools.

PROCRASTINATION

> *Any opportunity to do something is also an opportunity not to do it.*
>
> —Eli Josel

Let's get something out of the way right away. Everyone procrastinates. All the kids are doing it! So take some comfort in the fact that you're not alone.

One 2014 study found that a whopping 80 to 95 percent of college students procrastinated on a regular basis, particularly when completing assignments and coursework. And their high school counterparts? Not that far behind. Research—and there is a lot—shows that all this procrastinating makes you feel stressed and anxious and negatively impacts your grades.

So with all that said, why the heck do you do it? Why is it so difficult to activate or stay motivated when the consequences you're suffering are so negative?

As an academic/life coach for teens and college students for the past fifteen years, not a day goes by where I am not coaching, emailing or working with a student on overcoming their procrastination.

Here are a few insights I've gained along the way:

For some of you, the act of getting started is just too difficult and overwhelming. What you want to accomplish feels too big or vague.

For others, it's the lack of structure or immediacy. Without a

schedule or deadline, you just can't muster enough energy to start . . .
or finish.

Some tasks seem boring, mind-numbing or wastes of time. For
some, you just don't give a crap. (Your words, not mine.)

Some of you lack a *time sense*, an ability to know how long
it takes to get something done. I've heard too many stories from
students starting to work on a six-page research paper two hours
before it's due.

Some of you simply don't know how to study and therefore don't.

For others, the fear of failure, disapproval or imperfection stops
you right in your tracks.

And then there are those of you who can't keep the distractions at
bay. (You know who you are!)

As you can see, I've heard and seen it all! And I've read and
researched a ton on this topic. What I've come to learn is that
procrastination, especially why we do it, is multilayered and complex.
It's not as simple as believing that it's a deep character flaw or that
you're just lazy. If it only were that simple!

Let me explain.

Procrastinating doesn't necessarily make you a procrastinator.
Think about it. We all put things off from time to time. We all
waste time. Heck, we also don't always finish what we started. And
sometimes it's not horrible or detrimental to our well-being. And it all
works out in the end. Feel better?

Not all procrastination looks the same. There is a huge
difference between delaying doing something until the very last
minute and still getting it done vs not doing it at all and suffering the
consequences for it.

**Students procrastinate (for the most part) for different
reasons than adults do.** I know you're angry and tired of being
told what to do. All. The. Time. You feel powerless and you'd like
some control.

Just because you procrastinate doesn't mean you're lazy. (OK,
maybe sometimes. But aren't we all?) Or stupid. Or weak. And you're

definitely not hopeless. No matter what anyone has told you. (And I know you've heard them all, so I feel for you on this point.)

Different types of procrastination need different tools to help manage them. (More on that as we dive deeper into the book.)

You can be a functional procrastinator. Yes, there is such a thing. Or at least I think so.

For some of you, waiting until the last minute works. It gets you activated and stops you from all that waffling back and forth. You stay uberfocused, get done what you need to get done and feel your creative juices flowing freely. It simply works for you.

I don't believe that you can "cure" your procrastination. What I do believe is that with the right tools and strategies, you can absolutely learn to manage it. (This is where my expertise comes in handy!)

We don't always realize what is getting in our way, or worse, we assume our roadblocks are something they're not. In my experience, the key to managing your procrastination is to truly understand why you do it in the first place. That's not easy, I know. I can throw all kinds of tips, tools, strategies and systems at you to combat your procrastination, but none of them will be truly effective until you understand your roadblocks.

Take a look at the following diagram. I'm thinking you'll recognize some of these categories. They are some of the more common reasons you procrastinate. As we move through the book, we're going to take a deeper dive into each one. By doing so, I hope you'll develop a clearer understanding of what's getting in your way,

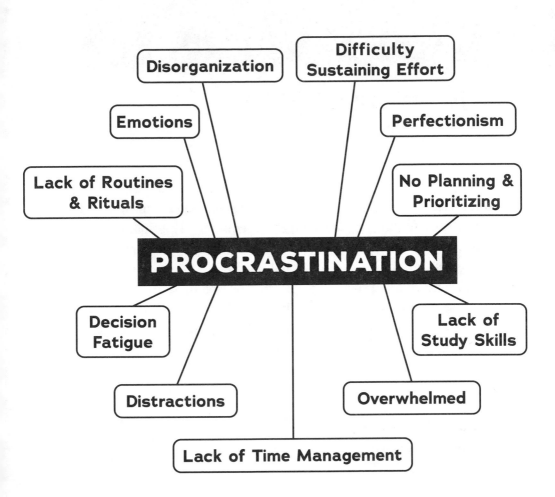

have a few "aha" moments as you recognize yourself in my students' stories and collect an arsenal of tools for getting down to business.

I also promise to keep it real. Offer no judgment. And make things as easy to understand as possible.

In other words, I'm going to show you how to do it now.

Chapter 1
"I HAVE TIME"

TIME MANAGEMENT

I could write a whole book just on the importance of learning how to manage time so that you can manage your procrastination. It's that important—because managing your time effectively can help you to feel in control and increase your productivity.

In all my years of coaching, the most heated debates and conversations about procrastination center on time management . . . or the lack of it. And it's the issue I get the most pushback on from you, including these kinds of mantras:

"I have everything under control."
"I'll deal with it next week when it comes."
"It will all get done in time."
"I won't forget to do it."
"It's on my radar."

And my personal favorite? "I've got plenty of time." Until you don't.

So I need to ask: How are those working out for you?

For some of you, it might be working out just fine. Maybe you never feel rushed and you have plenty of time to do your best work on every project. But for the others, I'm thinking you might need to learn some basic time management skills.

Here are a few time management takeaways my students have learned along the way:

1. There is NO way to stop procrastinating without focusing on time management. Usually they go hand in hand.
2. You need to be able to see your time to learn how to manage it. And you **do** need to learn how to manage it. Because no matter how much you think you have it under control, at some point you will have that "oh, shit" moment on a Sunday night when you realize your poli sci paper (or calc problem set or chem lab report) is due the next morning.
3. Time management is not just a **school** skill. (Do I have your attention now?) It's a **life** skill. No one is going to give a rat's ass if you studied for your Mesopotamia test in ninth grade. But your boss or clients or college professors will **absolutely** care if you are chronically late for meetings or deadlines or you don't turn in that proposal on time. And they won't care for the excuses that go along with it.
4. You need to know how long things take you to do, how quickly time is passing and how much time you have left.

So if you're ready to take the plunge, let's jump in. Time is ticking.

BUILDING A TIME SENSE

Do you really know how long things take you to do? Or how much time you have to get them done? For instance, how long does it take you to read a chapter in your English book? Or write a ten-page history paper?

The bottom line? To learn to manage your time, you must know how long it takes to get things done. There's no magic elixir here. Guessing that you think it may take you a certain amount of time to accomplish something is probably as accurate as throwing a dart at the wall blindfolded. And trying to guess actually **wastes** time. Kind of ironic, huh?

ESTIMATING TIME

Let's start with estimating time. Knowing how long it takes to make your breakfast, drive to school or take a shower is called having a *time sense*. Having that knowledge will help you set limits, plan, get started and stop procrastinating.

When I first start working with a student, I gauge their time sense by asking how long they think certain daily activities take them to do. Here's how that conversation usually goes:

Me: How long does it take to walk your dog?
Student: Twenty minutes.
Me: How long does it take you to make your lunch?
Student: About twenty minutes.
Me: How long does it take to walk across campus?
Student: Around twenty minutes.

See the pattern here? It doesn't matter what I ask. The answer seems to always come back to twenty minutes! What this immediately shows is that my student doesn't have a very well-developed time sense.

You can easily do this test yourself. On the next page are a series of questions to see how in tune you are with how long things take. Feel free to add some of your own and skip the ones that are irrelevant to you. Make sure to write down estimates before doing each one. Then time your tasks as you do them and compare the estimates to the actual time it took.

Notice that I didn't include any school-related questions. I want you to focus first on the activities you do on a regular basis, the ones that are super familiar to you and that don't cause you much stress or require much brainpower. That should make estimating time for your routine tasks a bit easier than estimating for your school activities. (We'll get to those next.)

> **Classroom Confessionals**
> **Biggest "Oh, Shit" Moment?**
> "Failing physics, the one class I needed to pass more than any other at school."
> —Jared, college junior

How Long Does It Take You To . . . ?

Activity	Estimated time	Actual time
Prepare breakfast		
Make lunch		
Walk your dog		
Care for your pet		
Take a shower		
Brush your teeth		
Watch your favorite video		
Watch your favorite TV show		
Listen to your favorite podcast		
Make your bed		
Do your laundry		
Empty the dishwasher		
Practice an instrument		
Text a friend		
Drive to school		
Walk to your first class		
Send an email		
Check Instagram/ Twitter/Snapchat		
Plan your outfit		
Blow-dry your hair		
Stop at your local coffee shop		

Your answers to these activities will be most helpful in understanding where you sit in relation to time. If everything seems to take about the same amount of time, your time sense could use some major improvement. And if you are pretty accurate in how long things take you, you can use that information to help build up your time sense for activities that are unfamiliar or that you don't do quite as often.

How did you do?

Let's move on to estimating school stuff, such as writing a paper, reading a chapter, working on textbook questions or rewriting your notes. If something is a multistep project such as completing a long term paper, first break down the steps and then try to estimate each one. So instead of estimating "write paper," your tasks would include such things as pick research topic, write thesis, choose five sources, take notes, create outline and so on.

This will be a LOT harder to do than your daily tasks. I know some subjects are harder for you than others. Or you might prefer one subject over another, which could cloud your estimates. Try to stay as objective as you can.

Write down estimates before doing each one, time your tasks and then compare the estimates to the actual time it took. Definitely do these exercises more than once! The more you record and see the difference between your estimated time and actual time, the better your time sense will become.

As you keep practicing, you'll learn to adjust your time estimates on similar assignments as well. That's the best part!

Use the form on page 17 to start estimating your time.

You can improve your time sense even further. Try drawing parallels by comparing an unknown period of time or an activity you don't often do to something very familiar. It might look something like this: "It took me thirty minutes to read two chapters in my English book, which is the same amount of time it takes me to listen to my favorite podcast." Tethering something you are unfamiliar with to something that you do all the time will help you gain a better understanding of how long things take.

What are some things you can compare your time to?

How Long I Think It Takes
vs
How Long It Really Takes

Activity	Estimated time	Actual time

MAPPING TIME

Now that you're on your way to developing a time sense, you're ready to start actually visualizing time. That's no easy task.

Think about it. You can't SEE or HOLD time in your hands, which makes time a very difficult concept to understand. It's pretty invisible to most of us.

Learning to see time in more tangible ways can help take its invisibility out of the equation. Here's one of my favorite student stories to illustrate my point:

MICHELLE'S STORY

Sixteen-year-old Michelle thought she had a major procrastination problem, but it turned out to be a time management issue instead. Michelle couldn't understand why she didn't have enough time to get a significant amount of homework done before leaving for swim practice each day. She was a star swimmer and had practice after school. Michelle also had to travel half an hour each way to get to practice.

By the time she got home in the evenings, showered and had dinner, she was facing mountains of homework. She was able to complete what was due the next day, but because of the late hour, she was putting off larger projects and studying.

When I first met with Michelle, she mapped out her after-school schedule for me. She left school at 2:45 p.m. and had to be at swim practice by 5:00. So in her estimation, she had about two hours to get her homework done.

Michelle had forgotten to take into account her travel time home, her responsibilities when she returned home, and even the time it took to leave class, gather what she needed for the evening and walk to her car.

However, I also knew that if I simply told her this, it would be hard for her to grasp. The point I wanted to make would be more realistic to her if she could "see" how she spent her time each day before practice. I had Michelle track how she spent that time for a week. It went something like this:

The Digital Download
RescueTime

This time-tracking app is a game changer! It records how and where you spend your time online. It analyzes EVERYTHING you do in a day, from which apps you use to how much time you spend on your favorite websites. (No hiding your time management habits here!) Consequently, if you want to seriously eliminate the distractions in your life and get work done faster, RescueTime is a great way to improve your time management game. And it can even temporarily block your go-to websites!

How Much Time Did Michelle Really Have to Get Her Homework Done?

School over	2:45 p.m.
Leave school for home	3:00 p.m.
Arrive home/Have snack	3:10 p.m.
Walk dog	3:30 p.m.
Change for swimming	3:45 p.m.
Homework	4:00 p.m.
Leave for swimming	4:30 p.m.
Arrive at swimming	5:00 p.m.

Two hours (she thought) vs thirty minutes (actually!)

Those two hours of homework time that Michelle thought she had was down to thirty minutes! Huge difference. We made some adjustments to Michelle's after-school schedule (she stopped coming home two days a week and did homework in the school library before practice) so she would have more time to complete assignments and bust that awful feeling of procrastinating.

Tracking how you spend your time over the course of a week or two is something you can easily do too. Some of my students say it's actually fun. (Notice I said *some!*)

TIME-TRACKING INSTRUCTIONS

1. Create a blank schedule grid on your computer, or visit HowToDoItNowBook.com to download this one.
2. Block out your "nonnegotiable" time—time spent in school or at your job, for instance.
3. If you have any free periods or free time between classes, make sure you mark those.
4. Fill in after-school activities, college events and other commitments that are already planned.
5. Block off your mealtimes, chores and self-care.
6. Next, accurately record how the rest of your time is spent by recording your activities in roughly half-hour increments.
7. Include social media, time spent with friends, binge-watching television or even procrastinating! No judgment.
8. Be truthful. The more honest you are, the easier it will be to see where your time is going.
9. Use the example Time Tracker to help you fill out yours.

Review the tracker. Is anything surprising? Did something take you way longer than expected? Are you spending time on stuff you don't mean to?

Or did you have free time in spots you didn't expect? Ideally, you'll have a better sense of where your time goes.

WEEKLY TIME TRACKER

TIME	Monday	Tuesday	Wednesday	Thursday	Friday	Saturday	Sunday
7:00 - 7:30	Yearbook Meeting	Guidance Counselor					
7:30 - 8:00							
8:00 - 8:30							
8:30 - 9:00							
9:00 - 9:30							
9:30 - 10:00							
10:00 - 10:30							
10:30 - 11:00			SCHOOL			Breakfast with Dad	
11:00 - 11:30							
11:30 - 12:00							
12:00 - 12:30							
12:30 - 1:00							
1:00 - 1:30							
1:30 - 2:00							Football Game
2:00 - 2:30						Homework	
2:30 - 3:00							
3:00 - 3:30	Tutoring	Yearbook Meeting	English Lab	Haircut	Shopping with Jill		
3:30 - 4:00							
4:00 - 4:30							
4:30 - 5:00	Homework	Homework	Homework				
5:00 - 5:30				Dance Class	Homework		
5:30 - 6:00							
6:00 - 6:30	Dance Class						
6:30 - 7:00							Dinner with Grandma
7:00 - 7:30			Play Rehearsal				
7:30 - 8:00							
8:00 - 8:30	Homework			Homework	Movies		
8:30 - 9:00					Maddie's Party		
9:00 - 9:30							Homework
9:30 - 10:00							

WEEKLY TIME TRACKER

TIME	Monday	Tuesday	Wednesday	Thursday	Friday	Saturday	Sunday
7:00 – 7:30							
7:30 – 8:00							
8:00 – 8:30							
8:30 – 9:00							
9:00 – 9:30							
9:30 – 10:00							
10:00 – 10:30							
10:30 – 11:00							
11:00 – 11:30							
11:30 – 12:00							
12:00 – 12:30							
12:30 – 1:00							
1:00 – 1:30							
1:30 – 2:00							
2:00 – 2:30							
2:30 – 3:00							
3:00 – 3:30							
3:30 – 4:00							
4:00 – 4:30							
4:30 – 5:00							
5:00 – 5:30							
5:30 – 6:00							
6:00 – 6:30							
6:30 – 7:00							
7:00 – 7:30							
7:30 – 8:00							
8:00 – 8:30							
8:30 – 9:00							
9:00 – 9:30							
9:30 – 10:00							

GOOD OLD-FASHIONED ANALOG CLOCKS

I'm assuming you know how to tell time. And that you probably even learned on an analog clock. But I'm also assuming that once the analog clock portion of your math lesson was over, you rarely looked at another old-fashioned clock again. Let's face it. It's a digital world. And we're all living in it. The thing is, a digital clock is not going to cut it if you really want to be able to see your time. Or plan it.

Why? Because time is three-dimensional. It has a past and a future. A beginning and an end. It moves continuously.

With a digital clock or watch you only see one aspect of time—the present. Go ahead and see for yourself. Grab your phone. I know it's next to you.

Look down at it. What do you see? Is it 4:26 p.m.? Or 8:52 p.m.?

So riddle me this, Batman: If all you see is one time and that time is the present time, how can you know how much time you have left? Or how much time has passed? Even how far along you are?

Think about it. You started working on your math homework at 5:05 p.m. You need to leave for work at 6:15 p.m. It's 5:43 p.m. Now answer the questions above.

Exactly. It's kind of hard to do without doing some math. And doing that math isn't always easy. And it takes time!

So what do we do about this? Easy fix. We hang analog clocks. **IN EVERY ROOM YOU SPEND TIME IN.** Including the bathroom. Especially the bathroom. And if you share a bathroom with siblings or in a college dorm, either invest in a small portable one OR get a waterproof watch with an analog face.

I know. I get a great deal of pushback on this. Most of my students say that they don't need a watch because they have a cell phone. But during class or while taking exams, you won't have access to your phone. And that is EXACTLY the time when a watch will come in handy!

Let's dive into WHY an analog is the only way to truly see time move.

An analog with its hands lets you see time move and therefore where you are in relation to the rest of your day. With an analog clock you can see the present time (where the hands are when you look at them), elapsed time (where the hands were at the beginning of a period and where they are in the present) and future time (how far the hands need to move to get to a time).

Seeing elapsed and future time helps you learn these concepts and better understand how long you have for tasks and how much time before a deadline.

ARE YOU SEEING THE FUTURE?

A crucial concept in time management is something called *time horizon*. This is basically how far you can look into the future to plan ahead. When you're a very young child, your time horizon is super short, about an hour or so. As you get older, it gets further away. This allows you to plan into the future.

Here's what I know. Most (not all) of you live in two worlds. The *now* and the *not now*. **Now** means right now. It could be 8:30 p.m. wherever you are, and you are just thinking about anything that is right in front of you . . . *now*. And then way over there (so far away you can't see it) is the *not now*. That's where your future lives. Two hours from now. Tomorrow. A week. Even six months.

> 😮 **Classroom Confessionals**
> **What's the largest assignment you've completed in the shortest amount of time?**
> "Pulled an all-nighter and wrote a whole six-page paper the day before it was due. It was probably garbage."
> —Casey, college sophomore

And sometimes what you have going on later in the day or later that week or month can affect what you need to do **NOW**.

This is called your *future awareness*.

The thing is, you not only need to be aware of things happening in the future, but you also need to **PLAN** for them. Which brings us right back to the procrastination dilemma.

A lack of future awareness is a huge factor that contributes to lateness with deadlines, homework and lots of other stuff. Without future awareness, it's nearly impossible to accomplish what you need to.

How do you develop future awareness? By seeing your time. And then planning it. We'll get into all of that in the planning chapter.

TIMELY TIPS

Are you feeling as if you're getting this time thing down? Good! Here are a few more tips to help you feel in control of your clock.

Use alarms and timers. They help you to focus on what is right in front of you—or what we call *present time*, by being in charge of your *future time*. If you need to be somewhere in thirty minutes, setting an alarm means you don't need to remember. The alarm does

SOUND THE ALARM!

Are you setting the same alarm sound for everything you do? Time to switch it up! Eventually, if you keep hearing the same old buzzing sound on your alarm, you're going to start ignoring it. Instead, change the sound of your alarm to signify different things. If you need to transition from hangout time to work time, use a quick loud sound to get into gear. And if it's time to get ready in the morning, a fast-paced song will create some much-needed energy to get you moving. Varying alarm sounds are more difficult to ignore and, therefore, will more likely get you going!

all the work for you! And if transitioning to the next activity gives you trouble, try setting multiple alarms to get you moving. When using a timer, I prefer visual timers over digital ones. Digital timers, such as kitchen timers, don't let you see time actually pass. A visual timer does. So as the allotted time winds down, you can easily keep track of how much is left.

And a tip within a tip? Set your timer for an odd number. Setting a timer for a typical amount of time—say fifteen or twenty minutes—is boring and unmemorable. Try seventeen or thirty-two minutes. Why? Because odd is different and different is fun and fun is memorable. It will provide you that extra kick to get you moving.

Work time over task. When you're told to "go finish your math homework before dinner" or your teacher says "Work on your science lab until class is over," can you see the end? Do you know what "done" looks like? Most students don't, and it leaves them feeling uneasy and procrastinating. Instead of sitting down to work with no end in sight, say, "I'll write for thirty minutes before dinner

Classroom Confessionals
Favorite food to eat while studying?
"Gum." —Marti, college junior

or I'll read for forty minutes before my next class." Being able to see a beginning, middle and end to your time will help you activate and procrastinate less. And you won't be staring down an endless tunnel of time.

And a tip within a tip? Use the Pomodoro Technique to help you work time over task. This popular time management method is really simple. Using a timer, you break down your work into twenty-five-minute chunks separated by short five-minute breaks. After about four Pomodoro rounds (if you need that many), you take a longer break of fifteen to twenty minutes.

Wear a vibrating reminder watch. It's a simple-to-use wristwatch that can be programmed to send you discreet vibrating reminders throughout the day. Most watches allow you to customize your own personalized reminders or preprogram one of theirs. You set the timer, and the watch vibrates and displays your reminder. A perfect way to keep on time and on task.

The Digital Download
Focus Booster
You can use the digital focus booster app to apply the Pomodoro Technique on any computer or download it to your phone. It helps you to overcome distractions, maintain focus and finish your work on time. I like it because it provides a deep understanding of your work cycles to improve your productivity. Pomodoro sessions are automatically recorded so you can review your output and track your time.

Chapter 2
"IT'S NOT DUE TILL FRIDAY"

HOMEWORK

Let's get right down to it. I know you hate homework. No surprise there. So it might be super easy to just equate the "I hate homework" excuse with the procrastination pushback I hear all the time and call it a day.

Oh, if it were that simple. But over the years I've gathered evidence of my own to figure out why you procrastinate about your homework or don't do it at all.

Here's what you tell me:

1. **My homework takes me too long to do.**
    I hear you! And the more homework you're assigned, the more you procrastinate.
2. **My assignments feel like busywork and are a waste of time.**
    You feel that the only purpose for homework is to get it done and that you don't actually learn anything or get anything out of doing it. I'm not even going to try to convince you otherwise.
3. **The assignments I'm given are one-size-fits-all.**
    You would like more say in the style in which you do it. Perhaps writing a straight-up essay to show your knowledge of the material is not your thing but crafting a song is. You all learn differently, and therefore, you should be able to complete homework in different ways.

4. **My teachers don't give me feedback.**
   "I don't need to do it because it's not graded."
   "He doesn't check to see if we did it so what's the point?"
   "Even if she collects it, we never get it back, so I have no idea what I got wrong."

   I'll leave a little room right here for you to write in a few more.

5. **I don't have a homework plan.**
   When I ask if you've given any thought to how you tackle your evening or week's homework, the answer is usually that you just sit down and do it . . . or don't.

   So where do we go from here?

HOW TO MAKE HOMEWORK HAPPEN?

First, I let you complain. Because I hate homework too. But not for the reasons that you may think . . . or for the reasons that you do. I'm all for homework that reinforces lessons taught in class, projects that can really speak to your creativity and learning styles, and assignments that challenge you as a critical thinker and problem solver.

I hate homework because most of you were never taught **HOW** to do it. Specifically, how to tap into your own unique, best practices to get homework done in an effective manner that enables you to get the most out of it. Because of that, an opportunity to learn lifelong skills is sorely missed.

Next, I tell you it's time to stop complaining. I'm all for a good pity party. But unfortunately, the way that homework is assigned is mostly out of your control because your teachers and professors, for the most part, are going to assign homework in the style that works for them. So, faced with that cold, harsh reality, eventually it's time to move on, stop procrastinating and get shit done.

To do that, though, you need to figure out how to make what you CAN control work for YOU in the best way possible.

Here are some time-tested ideas that truly work!

CREATE A PERSONAL HOMEWORK PROFILE

I know that homework is the last thing you want to do. So unless you figure out what your strengths and needs are and throw a little fun, energy and creativity in along the way, the "Not Now, Maybe Later" song will be playing all day long.

I'm guessing a lot of you are nodding but thinking, "OK. Great. But how do I figure that stuff out?"

Every one of you has individual homework preferences and personalities that, taken together, make up what I call a **Personal Homework Profile**. By tapping into these preferences and personalities, you can create a customized approach that focuses on YOUR best practices for getting work done. **It also takes the guesswork of "What worked for me before?" out of the equation.**

HOW TO GET STARTED

1. You can either use the chart I've included on the next page to document your homework experiences or feel free to create your own.
2. Note what strategies, tools, resources, spaces and other things you need to be more productive and on task.
3. Plan each type of work you do. For example, you might like doing your reading in a comfortable chair but need to spread out on the floor when working on a big project.

Let's do a deep dive into a few of the categories to show you how a **Personal Homework Profile** can be instrumental.

WHEN'S THE BEST TIME FOR ME TO WORK?

I get asked this question a lot. And there is no single right answer. Finding your best time will depend on when YOU feel your most productive based on your natural rhythm. Let me share a story with you.

PERSONAL HOMEWORK PROFILE™

Everyone has individual homework preferences & personalities. Tap into your best practices to create a customized approach to get your work done.

	Daily Homework	Studying for Exams	Papers/Projects	Reading
Energy Level: time of day				
Style: independent, group, body double				
Focus: multitasking vs one subject at a time				
Pace: fast & furious vs slow & steady				
Performance: make a plan vs spontaneous				
Deadlines: last minute vs long lead time				
Furniture: desk, floor, table, bed, chair				
Space: lights, windows, closed/open door				
Environment: small & cozy vs large & open				
Organization: revealer vs concealer				
Sound: quiet vs noise				
Music: instrumental, classical, current				
Necessary supplies: timer, calculator, index cards				
Homework tools: planner, apps, checklist				
Favorite foods:				

MADDIE'S STORY

Some of you want and need to start homework right after school.

That was my daughter, Maddie. When she was in high school, she would come home, not take off her coat, bypass the kitchen and head straight to her room to begin that evening's homework. This strategy worked for her because Maddie had **"attention residue"** left over after being in school all day. The material from the day was fresh. She felt as if she still had gas in her tank and could continue at full speed.

Also, Maddie's after-school activities were in the early evenings, and she preferred leaving for them knowing her work was completed. That mind-set was motivating and a stress reliever for her. The practice of getting work done immediately continued into college, where she would head straight to the library between her classes to get a jump start on assignments or to continue editing a paper. Working late into the night was too difficult for her. She equated waiting until the evenings with procrastinating, and that was anxiety producing.

However, for many others, starting homework right after or during school hours is ineffective and, in some ways, counterproductive. Let me give you another example.

JAKE'S STORY

It took Jake, a high school junior, hours to finish his homework. As I dove deeper into Jake's after-school routine and homework habits, I found that he was beginning his homework immediately upon arriving home. But Jake couldn't focus on his work during that time. He would get up, walk around, eat and find a million other reasons not to get started. Jake was also exhausted from the day. Put a fork in him. He was done!

Any of you ever feel that way?

Granted, more things were leading to the procrastination. But clearly, Jake needed downtime immediately after school so he could refill his gas tank. That enabled him to regain his focus so he could attend to his homework later on.

JOSH'S STORY

Finding your prime time doesn't only have to be about homework time. In Josh's case, it extended to his college class schedule too. Josh was a self-proclaimed procrastinator. He figured out that he did his best work at night. Why? During the day he felt no immediacy to get his work done. The day was long and he "had plenty of time." Sound familiar? However, once evening hit, he felt the clock ticking—and the need to race against it! Therefore, when Josh crafted his class schedule each semester, he avoided classes that met in the evening. He knew that was his prime time. And he wanted to protect that productive time from being "wasted" by sitting in class.

Not only will you have different times of day when you feel most productive, you will also find that you like working on different things at different times. Perhaps you need your early morning boost of energy to get that psychology paper started but prefer to do your reading for English literature later in the evening. Recognizing which times are most productive for which types of work is an important element to creating your **Personal Homework Profile**.

WHERE'S THE BEST SPOT FOR ME TO WORK?

Raise your hand if you think you need to work at a desk . . . in your room . . . with the door closed. Or in the campus library alone in the stacks. Or some version of that.

You're not alone. Most students resort to these environments by default. More likely their parents and teachers told them that those are the only "appropriate" places to work. And students were never taught about other options.

To be fair, for some, these traditional study spots work. But for most, the bedroom and library are the least effective places to get homework done. Let me tell you one of my favorite client stories to illustrate my point.

RYAN'S STORY

I met Ryan when he was a junior in high school. In his parents' eyes, he was a huge procrastinator. When it was time for Ryan to do homework, he opted to wander the house in search of his three younger siblings—a noisy bunch. His mom would redirect him to his bedroom, where it was quiet, so he could work . . . or at least try to.

On my initial visit to Ryan's house, I headed straight to his room. On the third floor, it was extremely quiet and secluded from the rest of the house. I asked Ryan if he liked doing homework there. Interestingly, Ryan told me he found it too quiet and isolated to concentrate. He said he gravitated downstairs because the noise generated by his siblings helped him feel connected, enabling him to relax and focus.

Tapping into his best practices, this is what we came up with: Ryan would do his homework on the kitchen table in the midst of all the commotion. He used an inexpensive tabletop presentation board that he could place on the kitchen table to give him some privacy. And he would wear earplugs or listen to music to drown out some of his brothers' noise. The only rule was that his brothers needed to ignore Ryan. With some other minor tweaks, Ryan was able to better initiate and complete his work.

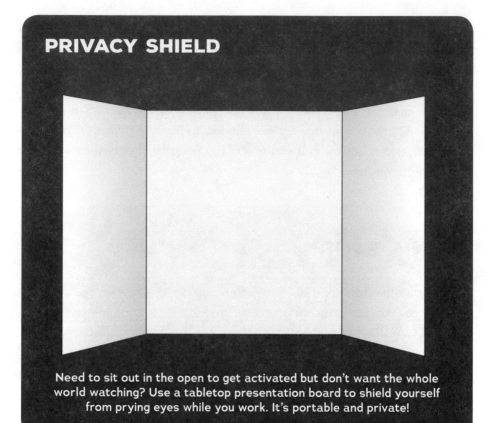

PRIVACY SHIELD

Need to sit out in the open to get activated but don't want the whole world watching? Use a tabletop presentation board to shield yourself from prying eyes while you work. It's portable and private!

While finding your one sweet spot at home or on campus can feel like a major win, finding several is a true victory. One of my favorite exercises to do with my college students is called Pick Your Places. At the beginning of each semester, I have them walk around campus and find five places where they would be comfortable getting work done. They can't include their dorm room or apartment, nor the main library on campus. It must be five unique places that they would not normally think of for working.

What's the point of finding five places?

Homework is boring. And doing it in the same place all the time can get very old very quickly. Changing your environment keeps things interesting and fresh just when you start to lose focus and attention. Pick Your Places becomes a list we refer to again and again, especially knee-deep into the semester when the procrastination bug sets in.

The more out of the box you can go, the better. The campus coffee shop or dorm lounge are great choices, but the photography darkroom or music rehearsal studio are even better.

And a tip within a tip? Don't forget outdoor spaces to clear your head and get you going. Sometimes a favorite tree (think Rory Gilmore from *Gilmore Girls*) or a view of a lake is all you need to get moving.

WHAT DO I DO IF I CAN'T SIT STILL?

Is it too hard for you to sit still to get work done? Do you feel the urge to switch locations to keep your effort level up? Let me introduce you to Rachel.

RACHEL'S STORY

When doing homework, Rachel bored easily and procrastinated frequently. Therefore, any ideas and strategies I came up with needed to be fun and full of energy for her to get excited about them. She also needed to move around a lot to focus. Using some of my teachings about learning and movement, I created the game Hide the Homework for Rachel to try.

When Rachel came home from school, I had her gather all her books, supplies and homework for the evening and separate them into piles by subject. Then without her looking, I hid her homework in various locations around her house. That first day, chemistry went into her bathtub (with no water, of course), English vocabulary under the kitchen table, math inside the walk-in pantry closet and so on. Wherever she found her homework was where she had to do it. Rachel loved this game. By adding an element of surprise into her daily homework routine, she was able to stay motivated and on task.

Before you start with the whole "That's great, but I'm not going to ask anyone at home or college to hide my homework for me. I'm not twelve," I totally get it and have an answer for that! You can still get the same benefits if YOU place different subjects in different rooms in your house or plan to change locations every so often while you study on campus. Just make sure it's one subject to one place. Although you won't be surprised by where your homework landed, you'll still get that much-needed energy boost of moving around to maintain focus and attention.

BEAT THE CLOCK

Do you find yourself reading the same paragraph over and over and realizing you have no idea what you read? Is your mind drifting off

BED OR NO BED

I get it. I really do. I like my bed too. But I'm not quite sure if I am on the doing-work-in-bed bandwagon. The bottom line is that I don't give a crap where you do your homework, as long as you do it! And some of you can and will get your work done in your bed. Under the covers and all! But most of you don't. And for some very real reasons. One, the coziness of your bed and the other activities it is suited for cause a real procrastination problem. Because if you have a choice of working on your macroeconomics or binge-watching Netflix or scrolling through your Instagram feed or even napping, we know what you're going to do. Two, there is a very real possibility that you will eventually associate your bed with your schoolwork and all the not-so-happy feelings that go along with that. And in extreme cases, that can lead to sleep issues. So if you really need to spend time buried in your bed doing some schoolwork, save it for your light reading and don't try to tackle your heavy-duty assignments from under the covers. Is that a reasonable compromise?

The Digital Download
To-Do List Apps

So many task management apps can capture our to-do lists that it's hard to know which one to choose. I've got you covered! Here are my students' top two choices:

Remember the Milk. This app takes a lean and fast approach to task management, which is the main reason why my students gravitate to it. You just add your tasks in plain text, organize them into lists and you're done. Its clean design means there are no extra features (no distracting graphics) to navigate through. It shows you the tasks you need to do today, tomorrow, as well as any that are overdue, right when you open the app. No searching needed. The app also includes due dates, along with priorities on tasks so you know what your most important responsibilities are!

Added plus? The app syncs with all your devices, integrates with your emails, talks to Siri, and lets you attach documents, photos and the like to your tasks.

Todoist. What sets this one apart from all the other to-do list apps out there? First, it is free! And what student doesn't like to hear those words (parents too!)? Second, it's available on all devices and platforms, making using it a breeze. (Hello from Grandma's house!) But the biggest reason I hear? Its distraction-free design allows you to be super detailed with your tasks. You can add tasks to projects, add due dates, set priorities by color and order and create recurring tasks. Lastly, the app is ridiculously easy to use.

after working on one subject for a while? Research has found (I know, I promised you only a few mentions of research!) that switching subjects helps you to stay focused. Here's how my game Beat the Clock can help.

Like Hide the Homework, you separate your homework into piles by subject in Beat the Clock. But instead of placing it in different locations to complete, you set up workstations around a table. Biology at one chair, foreign language at another and so on. The key to this game is to also set a timer to work on one subject for a limited amount of time. Start at one station and once the timer goes off, finish whatever math problem or lab question you are working on and move on to the next station and subject. You move from station to station until all your work in all subjects is completed.

The point here is that by switching subjects continuously, you are less likely to drift off and lose focus. Giving yourself the mental break from working on one subject area by starting another is the key to procrastinating less.

SHOULD I TAKE BREAKS?

Short answer? Yes, you should. Working intensively for a short period of time and then taking a break helps you learn more. But there's a right way and a wrong way. You want your breaks to be energizing and productive. And not too long.

SEVEN SMART STRATEGIES FOR BETTER BREAKS

SET a timer to work for no more than an hour. Beyond that the law of diminishing returns kicks in.

STICK to a plan. Determine how you're going to spend your breaks and for how long.

SOCIAL media. Keep it short and sweet.

STEP away from your study area. Go for a walk . . . but not toward the television.

STRETCH your muscles.

SWITCH your study location.

SNACK Sip. Swallow. Repeat.

FAVORITE SPACES AND PLACES TO MAKE HOMEWORK HAPPEN

Under the kitchen table	Toilet
Back seat of the car	Bathtub
Sitting in the shower	Laundry room
Closet floor	Coffee shop
Local library	Religious school
Bagel store	Attic
Backyard	Local park
Pizza place	School bus

SHOULD I LISTEN TO MUSIC?

Scientists, researchers, teachers, parents and even you have endless conversations on whether listening to music while doing homework is beneficial. Some research studies say that certain types of music can be distracting and even impede a student's recall and memorization. Others have demonstrated the benefits of music in helping the brain activate. They say that music bolsters attention and focus.

Truthfully, it really doesn't matter what anyone says. Because the only thing that matters is whether YOU need it and when. Some of you need it to drown out distracting sounds around you. Others need it to get their adrenaline going to get motivated. Some find that the rhythm of the music they listen to provides a rhythm for the work they are doing. And still others need music to soothe and calm their brain while working on a difficult subject. Whatever the case may be, if you need music to chill, initiate, focus or pace, then let's make sure you are "doing" music right.

MAKE A HOMEWORK PLAYLIST!

This is hands down one of my absolute favorite anti-procrastination tools for students!

Here's what you need to do:

Create a forty-five-minute (more or less) playlist with songs on it that you like and are familiar with. Make sure that you don't include any new music. If your favorite artist or group just dropped a new album, don't include that music because you might get too focused on the music itself at the expense of focusing on your work.

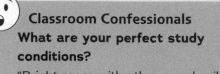

Classroom Confessionals
What are your perfect study conditions?
"Bright room with other people silently working too." —Marti, college junior

The key is to pick songs you love and can listen to on a loop, but won't have you singing and dancing in the library.

When it's time to get down to homework, just switch on your playlist and you're ready to (literally) rock! Feel free to make several playlists if that works best for you. I have students who have a playlist for each of their subjects or a playlist for shallow vs deep work. Just customize it to your needs. It's as easy as that.

Here's why it works:

- Playing the same playlist every time you sit down to work eliminates the distraction of changing songs on your desktop or portable device. I always say it's the Spotify switch up that's distracting, not listening to the tunes.
- Since you're listening to the same music over and over, eventually the music becomes background noise and, hopefully, you'll focus on it less and less.
- Your playlist becomes an activation device. Don't you hear certain music and it elicits a response? I know when I hear my disco, I'm ready to hop on the treadmill or spin bike. It's the same with your homework. When you hear your playlist, it'll send a signal that it's time to get into work mode.

Classroom Confessionals
Favorite food to eat while studying?
"Ritalin."
—Jared, college junior

THE PERFECT PLAYLIST

Need some help putting together the perfect playlist? Here are some of my students' favorite suggestions:

Ambient 1: Music for Airports by Brian Eno

Beethoven's Symphony No. 6 in F Major, Op 68

Drukqs by Aphex Twin

Final Fantasy VII soundtrack by Nobuo Uematsu

"First Tube" by Phish

Grateful Dead at the Spectrum in Philadelphia 9/21/72

Innerspeaker, Lonerism, and *Currents* by Tame Impala

In the Court of the Crimson King by King Crimson

"In the Hall of the Mountain King" by Edvard Grieg

Interstellar by Hans Zimmer

Kid A by Radiohead

Koyaanisqatsi and *Music for 18 Musicians* by Philip Glass

Any LCD Soundsystem

"Lofi hiphop radio—beats to relax/study to" from Chilled Cow on YouTube

Maggot Brain by Funkadelic

Oxygène by Jean-Michel Jarre

Any Pink Floyd

"Take Five" by Dave Brubeck

Twin Fantasy and *Teens in Denial* by Car Seat Headrest

The Way Up by Pat Metheny Group

Z and *It Still Moves* by My Morning Jacket

- It's portable! Whether you are on the bus after the away game, at Grandma's eightieth birthday party, the dentist or the fraternity house, you always have it with you. No excuses!
- I saved the best for last! Your music can become a timekeeper. I have students who have been using playlists for so long that they know hearing a certain song means that they are twenty minutes in or that they're in the home stretch. Letting

the music create a time sense allows you to pause and pace yourself as you work.

A FEW MORE HOMEWORK HELPERS

While the **Personal Homework Profile** is intended to help you create a holistic approach to homework, here are some very specific homework helpers that can help you kick that procrastination to the curb. Again, the details and specifics of how you will use any of these are completely up to YOU!

Schedule daily homework time. Even if you have no homework on any given evening, you can use that time to get ahead in your reading, make up missed work, work on an extra credit project or begin reviewing notes for an exam. This consistency will help you build your homework habit.

Simplify your supplies. How does this affect procrastination? In every way! It's super easy to get overwhelmed by the amount of papers, sheets, handouts and everything else that takes over your school life. If you use one master binder or a few folders to corral your papers, you have to look for things in fewer places. Which means less time wasted looking for things. That means you have some energy left to do what you need to do. Otherwise, you're using up all your energy and focus to find what you need. Does that make sense? We'll dive much deeper into this in the organizing chapter.

Make a homework plan. Even if you write down your homework in a planner (more on that in the planning chapter) or check your syllabi nightly, I still want you to write out a to-do list every night. Specifically, write the order of how you are going to tackle your assignments. For some students, I suggest putting the hardest or

Classroom Confessionals
Favorite food to eat while studying?
"I don't eat. It's distracting." —Jeremy, college freshman

The Digital Download
Brain.fm

Are you craving music that scientifically **helps you focus when you're working or studying?** Then look no further than Brain.fm! This app uses an idea called dynamic attending theory, which suggests that certain rhythms and tone patterns can help your brain focus. Just open the app and tap on the listening mode you want, and music starts playing. Options include focus, sleep, recharge, and meditation. **Focus mode** is great for when you're trying to get and stay in the zone. My students swear by it.

longest task at the top and doing that one first, when you have a full tank of gas. You'll feel a sense of accomplishment after tackling the hardest to-do. For those who truly procrastinate, I recommend doing the smallest and easiest task to get you started. For most, doing a combination of both is best.

My student Hannah loved to mix it up. She would start off with the easiest assignment to get herself going and then tackle the hardest assignment next. When she was finished, she went back again to an easy one as a reward. No matter which method you choose, the most important thing is to make a plan. By actively committing to what you are going to do and when, you are more likely to accomplish what you've committed to do.

Get active. Put energy into your homework tasks by standing up to read or walking the dog while you review your notes. My son always studied his scripts and memorized his lines for school plays while pacing back and forth in our living room with his book in hand. Research shows that the more we move, the more our brain "lays down its learning."

Chapter 3
"I READ OVER MY NOTES"

STUDY SKILLS

DON'T TURN THE PAGE!

I know you're about to, but I promise this chapter will go down easy. Or as easy as a chapter about studying can!

So where do we begin?

First, we're going to spend a short time exploring the **WHY**, or "Why do you put off studying or not do it at all?" We'll lay out some of the obstacles that get in your way so you can try to identify the sources of your procrastination problems.

Then we're going to jump into the **HOW**, meaning "How can you study more efficiently and effectively?" I'll teach you tips, techniques, strategies and skills, and give you an arsenal of tools to use when it's time to get down to business.

So here's the God's honest truth—I had a really hard time starting this chapter. I wanted to come up with something witty that would catch your attention. Even I know that a chapter about study skills can have that kind of effect on students! So I searched the internet for articles on how to overcome procrastination when studying to get some creative ideas.

And here's the interesting bit. Every single article offered the same five tips—limit your distractions, find a quiet place, break down your tasks, make a study plan and take effective breaks. All solid tips. I even mention a few in the homework chapter. On a scale of one to ten, I'd give them definite eights.

What was glaringly missing and what should have been the number one tip in all these articles is *learn HOW to study*. I think that tip was missing because the authors all assume you know how to study. But you know that most of you really don't. And unless you know **HOW** to actually sit down (or lie down or stand up or walk around) and study, none of the suggestions listed on the previous page are going to work. And that procrastination plague is going to stick around for a really long time.

WHY YOU PUT OFF STUDYING

Here's what I'm hearing from you:

1. **I don't know how.** No surprise here. It doesn't matter if you're sixteen or twenty, go to public or private high school, a small liberal arts college or a Big Ten university. The actual steps needed for effective studying are lost on you. So you try to devise a few of your own strategies and clearly those just don't work. (More on that in a little bit.)

    While this might be the number one reason for most, you've shared plenty of others with me over the years.

2. **There's no due date.** Some would argue that there is a due date since there's a date for an actual test or quiz. That's true. But you also remind me that since there is no actual due date for studying in the days and weeks before a test or quiz, then there's no incentive to plan or study in advance (the day before the test) or to study at all.
3. **My studying is not graded.** Again, your test IS graded. But since your process or, to put it another way, your study *methods* or *tools* aren't graded, it's very easy to disconnect the two. Grades, for a million reasons, are a very powerful motivator. Wouldn't it be great if part of your test score included how well-thought-out your study guide was or how brilliantly creative your mock textbook page looked? Wouldn't that up the studying ante just a bit? I thought so!
4. **I was taught how to study, but those methods don't work for me.** Remember the homework chapter? You all learn differently, and

therefore, you should be able to study differently. The good news is that you have more wiggle room when it comes to studying. Just because your teacher or professor offers boring methods or ones that don't work for you, it doesn't mean you have to use them. It's your job to come up with methods that work for you.

5. **I don't know how to get started.** When I ask if you've given any thought to how you plan out your studying (what to do first, what tools you need), I get crickets. Or I hear that you just sit down and try to do it . . . or don't try at all.

6. **It's too vague, too big, or too overwhelming.** It doesn't matter how you dress it up. If your studying isn't broken down into manageable parts that you can wrap your brain around AND you don't understand what you are being asked to do, you aren't going to do it. It's as simple as that.

THE STUDY GUIDE SHUFFLE

Study guides are an old study tool standby. Here's a way to make them fun and fresh again! Follow my step-by-step process for taking your teacher's study guide to the next level.

- When handed a study guide in class, either grab extra copies or copy on your own. If neither is an option, retype it from scratch.
- Fill out the first copy using your notes, textbook and old tests and quizzes. Review it and then put it aside.
- Fill out the second copy from memory! Highlight what you didn't know.
- Practice what you didn't know and finish the second guide. Repeat until it is completed.
- Cut the third guide into question strips. Put questions into a box or basket.
- Shuffle the box, pick a question and test yourself again.

When I work with students to demonstrate the difference between a manageable task vs a vague assignment, I use this great exercise. Feel free to play along at home.

Let's say your math homework for the evening is, "Go to page 52 in your textbook and complete questions 1 through 5." Most of you would tell me you understand the instructions. You know EXACTLY what is expected of you. And since you do, you find it easy to turn to page 52 and get started. (Remember, this is not about whether you can do the math assigned but whether you understand the instructions.) That's because these instructions are specific, concrete and task-oriented. You see a beginning and an end.

Let's change it up. It's Monday night, you have a history exam on Thursday and your assignment for the evening is to "continue studying." Have I hit a nerve? Who likes assignments like that? Basically, no one. Because what does "continue studying" mean? How do you know if you've succeeded at the assignment? You really can't. And so, faced with a task you can't measure, the procrastinating part of you is on full display.

So if I changed the assignment from "continue studying" to "create study guide" or "review notes on the cultural aspects of ancient Mesopotamia," would you have an easier time getting started? Bingo! It's much easier to start on something when you can see the steps to the finish line!

7. **I hate the word *study*.** To the point where it gives you such a visceral reaction that you feel nauseated or you simply shut down.

I'll let you in on a little secret. I rarely use the word *study* when I'm working with my students. Why? Because that little five-letter word sends you all into such a tailspin that procrastination paralysis comes out in full force.

I've learned that when I switch out the word *study* for a word that resonates with you, your mind-set switches too. Let me explain.

ALANA'S STORY

When I first met Alana, a senior in high school, she was juggling a very heavy course load filled with AP classes, homework, play rehearsals, field hockey practices and all the stuff that goes with being a senior. Alana was also a very responsible and goal-oriented student. She had no problem completing homework that was due the next day. She got herself up and ready for school on time, rehearsed and practiced her lines without any prompting, and showed up for field hockey suited up and ready to run her drills. So where was the breakdown? When it came time to study. There was that word again. It stopped her in her tracks, paralyzing her. She simply couldn't activate.

As I dove deeper into my work with Alana, I found that she liked going to practice and rehearsal as it meant she was improving her skills. Working toward a goal. Then it hit me. Wasn't practicing the same as studying? When you study, aren't you trying to get better at understanding a specific subject? Aren't you working toward a specific goal? By reframing it in a way that made sense to Alana and using verbiage that she was familiar with, we were able to change her mind-set and get her unstuck and started.

PRACTICE VS STUDY

Here's why the word *practice* truly makes perfect!

1. **It means to get better at something.** You understand that when you have sports practice or play rehearsal or even music lessons and are told to practice, it's so you can get better at whatever it is you're learning.
2. **There's a process to follow.** Whether it's sports practice or play rehearsal, there's a process in place. Steps to follow. And when there's a plan or steps, it's much easier to get started . . . and finish.
3. **It's results-oriented.** You see the progression. And therefore you see your success. And success breeds success. And therefore helps you stay motivated.

4. **There's a beginning, a middle, and an end.** Don't discount this one. It's huge. You all like to know where to begin, where you are in the process and when it's going to end. When you show up for basketball practice or piano lessons, you know! And when you know, you're more likely to get moving.
5. **It becomes a habit (my favorite!).** When you do something every day, you get used to it. It becomes familiar. You stop thinking about it. It just becomes muscle memory. That works for studying too.

Over the years, I've replaced words like *study* or *review* with words like *create*, *move*, or even *play*, which help to promote action and get you moving.

They just have a much different feel to them. Don't you think? Tell me, which sentence motivates you more?

"Go study for your exam." Or *"Practice your vocabulary for your psychology midterm."*

HOW DO YOU STUDY?

Some of you might be saying, "Sure, I procrastinate sometimes, but I know how to study. I'm good!"

Really? Let's play a little game.

Here's a list of the most commonly used study strategies, in no particular order. From the list below, pick the study method you use the most often **OR** the one you think is the most effective for you.

Rewriting notes
Flash cards
Rereading your notes or textbook
Making outlines or study guides
Highlighting textbook
Self-testing
Studying in a group
Doing practice problems or questions from textbook

WHAT'S IN YOUR STUDY TOOLBOX?

Need some ideas to infuse your studying with creativity? Here are some of my students' favorite study tools broken down by different learning modalities. Add your favorites to the list!

SEE	HEAR	SAY	DO
Charts	Watch videos	Teach one another	Giant sticky notes
Photos	Class discussions	Study groups	Mock textbook page
Timeline	Podcasts	Review sessions	Flash cards
Graphs	Different teacher		Songs
Pictures			Study guides
Website			Mock tests
Mind map			Chapter questions

Which one did you choose?

According to a study done by Jeff Karpicke and his colleagues on the study strategies of students at Washington University in Saint Louis, over 83 percent of those students polled chose . . . wait for it . . . rereading your notes or textbook.

Any guesses as to why? Because it's an easy way out. Rereading is super passive. It takes no effort, which is why most of you do it. (Please don't be insulted.) But it's not very effective.

What's the most effective study method? It's actually self-testing! Asking yourself questions to make sure you have a deeper understanding of the material. And according to this study, only about 10 percent of students polled use this method.

So why don't more of you do it?

Because asking all those questions to truly understand what you are studying requires some serious heavy mental lifting. And that extra effort to go beyond just memorizing facts and figures requires you to push yourself, work a little harder and dig a little deeper to truly understand what you are learning. It hurts a little . . . or in some cases, it hurts a lot. And for most of us, our fallback position is to avoid pain at all costs.

Now does it make sense?

A wise professor once told me, "There is no learning without pain." And that's the step that most of you are missing.

It has got to hurt to work.

DO THIS, NOT THAT

If you seriously want to kick procrastination to the curb, then you need to learn some serious study strategies. Let's take a look at some common practices and see how we can tweak them to make them more effective.

ARE YOU PULLING ALL-NIGHTERS OR CRAMMING HOURS BEFORE YOUR EXAMS?

Try spacing out your studying. We're better able to recall information and concepts if we learn them in multiple, spread-out sessions. Think thirty-minute study sessions over a few days instead of a three-hour crash course the night before. Pressuring your brain because you procrastinated rarely works.

Classroom Confessionals
Biggest "Oh, Shit" Moment?
"Losing my academic scholarship." —Sam, college senior

ARE YOU REVIEWING YOUR NOTES ONCE AND THINKING YOU'RE READY FOR YOUR EXAM?

Repetition. Repetition. Repetition. For optimum studying you need to rinse and repeat. A lot.

ARE YOU USING JUST ONE STUDY TOOL?

If you think that creating a study guide and ONLY a study guide is the right approach (Hello, Quizlet!), then think again. Mix it up. Try different study tools to optimize your learning. It will keep it fresh and fun. And fresh and fun means you'll procrastinate less.

ARE YOU HIGHLIGHTING YOUR TEXTBOOK?

Picture this. You're sitting down to read a chapter. For the first time. With a highlighter in hand. Ready to highlight what you think is important to review later on. But answer me this: If you're reading material for the first time, how exactly do you know what is important (and should be highlighted) and what isn't (and should be left alone)? Especially when the material you're reading is difficult or dense. Answer? You DON'T!

The Digital Download
Quizlet

Quizlet, available through either its app or website, is like the mother ship calling you home! It lets you create your own flash cards (a fab tool for helping you memorize important facts and figures for exams) or use ones made by other students (which is exactly how my son got through AP government his senior year)! It has live games, more than three hundred thousand study sets and claims that over 90 percent of students who use its resources report higher grades. It's no wonder they have over fifty million users a month! I would drink their Kool-Aid too!

The Digital Download
SimpleMind

I'm a big believer that everyone learns differently! And many of my students love mind mapping, although it's not something I can do easily. SimpleMind helps you organize your thoughts by creating mind maps, which can then be seamlessly synchronized across multiple platforms and shared with others. It allows you to add photos, videos and even voice recordings. My students especially like that they can customize the appearance of their mind maps and select different layouts.

Try reading the chapter all the way through to get a feel for the material. THEN go back and highlight what you think is essential to know.

And a tip within a tip? Before you put highlighter to paper, make sure you can first answer the question, "Why is this important for me to know?"

ARE YOU JUST REREADING YOUR LECTURE NOTES?

News flash! Rereading doesn't make information stick. Instead, it becomes a path to developing a false sense of security where you think you truly understand what you're (re)reading when you don't. The reason for this is fairly obvious. When you reread something, you tend to do it with an "I know this!" mentality because the material is familiar. Therefore, you stop processing what you're reading, and you are no longer deepening your understanding of the material.

Instead of rereading, try re*writing*. Rewrite your lecture notes. The physical act of writing actually helps you absorb what you're reading on a much deeper level than reading the same material. To take it up a notch, when you rewrite, do it in a DIFFERENT manner from your original set. Draw a diagram, create an outline, develop a Q and A, anything that changes your notes into a different format. By organizing the material differently, you'll figure out whether you truly understand it. Or not.

ARE YOU ASKING, *WHY? HOW? WHAT?*

Whether reading your textbook, reviewing your notes, or even reading a novel for class, ask yourself these question starters. They will help you understand the material on a much deeper level.

BONUS! It's not bad if you can't always answer these types of questions. If you get one wrong or don't know an answer, that gives you a pretty clear picture of what you know and what you don't and, therefore, points you to what you need to work on.

ARE YOU READING A TEXTBOOK CHAPTER WITHOUT CHECKING OUT THE QUESTIONS AT THE END?

Just plain no! The questions at the end of each chapter are study gold! They basically do the work for you. So grab your notebook, write out each question, leaving space in between, and begin answering each question as you make your way through the chapter. Use the questions as a road map to help you find the important "landmarks" along the way. I find that this technique helps my students overcome their procrastination every time!

And a tip within a tip? Don't forget about the questions or highlighted text IN each chapter. General rule: If something is bolded, italicized or highlighted, you need to know it.

ARE YOU USING YOUR SAME OLD BORING STUDY TECHNIQUES?

Stop draining your brain and get active! Write a song to learn your Chinese, draw cartoon pictures to memorize your ancient gods, make up a dance routine to learn the periodic table. Anything to put some energy and fun into the process. More Active = More Engaged.

ARE YOU FOOLING YOURSELF INTO THINKING YOU KNOW IT WHEN YOU REALLY DON'T?

Oh, come on. I know and you know that when you kind of, sort of, maybe know some of the material, you pretend you really know it all so you don't have to deal with it. Not knowing things makes us all uncomfortable. And we tend to avoid that at all costs. So here's what I want you to do instead.

Stop studying in order. Think about it. It doesn't matter whether you are starting at the beginning of the year when studying for finals or the beginning of the chapter when studying for a big unit test. Studying in order leads to a false sense of security.

Follow me. Let's say you're reviewing the periodic table and you are reviewing the elements in the order they are laid out on the chart. You might really understand all the components to the elements oxygen and neon but are unsure of fluorine. Or "I know number one and I know number three but am unsure of two, so I'll just move on because knowing one and knowing three probably means I really do know two." See how that works? What to do instead? Mix it all up. Start in the middle. Jump around. Break up the order. Just stop hiding behind door number three.

Classroom Confessionals
What are your perfect study conditions?
"Nighttime. No stopping and starting. And lots of snacks."
—Amanda, college junior

And a tip within a tip? (I'm full of them today!) If the material you're reviewing requires you to study in chronological order, then review it backward. Yup! I learned this tip from a professor during my college years. We tend to spend way more time at the beginning of the textbook chapter, the professor's slide deck or even our own notes. By starting at the end and working our way backward, we guarantee that we've given everything equal time.

ARE YOU SPENDING THE SAME AMOUNT OF TIME STUDYING THE THINGS YOU KNOW AND THE THINGS YOU DON'T?

Here's an idea. When you start to review for an exam, feel free to put aside the things you know like the back of your hand. I hear from my students that the sheer volume of what they need to study can put them into procrastination paralysis. So by immediately eliminating from your pile what you know, you'll lighten the load and only have to focus on what is giving you trouble. Just remember to bring everything back out the night before for a quick review.

ARE YOU WORKING ALONE?

Time to call in the troops. There's no better procrastination buster than studying with others. It's literally one of the most effective study tools out there because it's loaded with all the good stuff.

- You're teaching one another vs just memorizing. And to teach is to know.
- You're talking out loud. It slows you down, helps you process and forces you to say it in a way that makes sense to you!

- You're writing on interactive whiteboards, quizzing one another, making up mock test questions—all the stuff that puts activity into your learning.
- You're drawing from one another's expertise. Meaning someone might be a math god, while another is a computer science whiz. Take advantage of all that knowledge.
- It keeps you accountable and, therefore, keeps that pesky procrastination at bay. Try getting up at 8 a.m. on a Saturday to study alone. Good luck with that. But if your study group is meeting at that time, trust me, you'll be on time. NO ONE wants to be that kid!

ARE YOU TAPPING INTO YOUR BEST PRACTICES WHEN STUDYING?

Flip back to the homework chapter and tap into the **Personal Homework Profile** you created. That's what it's there for.

ARE YOU DIVING IN WITHOUT COMMITTING TO THE WHAT AND WHEN?

We'll do a much deeper dive into planning strategies in that chapter. But here are two words I want you to remember: **Define and Assign**.

First, **DEFINE** what it is you need to study. Get specific. Remember the exercise we did at the beginning of the chapter? Here's where "learn the seven Mesopotamia gods and their importance to the ancient culture" is better than "study for my Mesopotamia test."

Next, **ASSIGN** when you are going to do it. Making appointments with yourself is a great way to motivate and not procrastinate. If you treat your studying with the same level of importance as an after-school activity or office hours with your professor, you are more apt to honor that commitment.

And a tip within a tip? Study **BEFORE** you do your evening's homework.

Let me tell you my client Molly's story.

MOLLY'S STORY

When I began working with Molly, she was having a difficult time studying for exams. Specifically, she was waiting for the night before to begin. Her intentions were good. She would write it in her planner and figure it into her daily plan. However, as a high school senior, Molly was super busy. She didn't arrive home each day until early evening. So by the time she decompressed, ate dinner and completed the homework that was due the next day, it was late into the night. By then Molly was exhausted. And it was too difficult for her to get her brain to do the heavy lifting that was required for studying. So if her test wasn't the next day, Molly gave herself permission to skip studying for that evening, thinking, "It can wait until tomorrow." But tomorrow never happened and Molly usually found herself staring down hours of studying the night before an exam. So to help kick this habit, I suggested to Molly she make one simple switch: Study *BEFORE* you do your nightly homework.

I know that most of you are saying that just feels weird or out of sync. It did for Molly too. At first, she resisted since it just didn't feel normal. But once she tried it, it actually worked. Molly operated on a system of have-tos and don't-have-tos. And I'm thinking most of you do too. Homework that was due the next day fell into the have-to pile. Studying for a test that wasn't the next day didn't. So by flipping it and studying first, Molly always completed her nightly homework as well, even if it was later in the evening. Molly also found that when she saved studying for last, it depleted her brainpower supply, leaving her with very little gas in her tank to get going. Switching it up resolved that issue for her.

ARE YOU THINKING "I'M NOT GOOD ENOUGH" OR "IT'S TOO HARD, SO WHY BOTHER?"

Nothing will have that train going full speed ahead on your procrastination track more than this self-defeating mantra playing over and over in your head. I get it. I firmly believe that high school is the only time in your life where there is an expectation that you need to be good at everything. And that is demotivating, to say the least. You do have some wiggle room when picking the college you attend or your college course schedule. When my son, Eli, was looking at colleges, he immediately ruled out any that had a math or language requirement.

But whether you are in high school or college, sometimes you will need to take a class that doesn't come easily to you. And that means you'll have to put in more effort, work hard, get help and exhaust all your resources. That's no easy task.

I want you to try changing the narrative in your head. Instead of saying "I don't get this," ask yourself, "How can I get this?" Or swap out "I don't know" with "What do I know?" And my favorite one? Changing "This won't work" to "What have I done previously that has worked?"

Chapter 4

"I DON'T NEED TO WRITE IT DOWN"

PLANNING

Every day I hear that you don't want to write things down, set up your time, create a plan or schedule to manage your workload, because "It takes too much time." But I also hear how strung out you feel. How far behind you are. How you forgot to do something important.

So let me see if I've got this straight: You'd rather constantly play catch up and rely on your not-so-perfect memory than take ten minutes to plan your schedule so you can feel more in control? Have you not realized that trying to remember what you have to do takes away from actually doing what you need to do?

No matter what you have on your plate—homework, studying, school activities, job, plans with friends, getting ready in the morning—you need to plan to make it happen. If you don't, you're bound to mess up. Make a mistake. Be late. Feel overwhelmed. Forget something. Stress out. Procrastinate.

But just because you know you **need** to plan doesn't mean that you know **how** to plan. That's what this chapter is all about.

THE BRAIN DUMP

The first step is to identify all the things you need to plan for. Sounds obvious, I know. But obvious doesn't necessarily mean easy. Especially because things you need to plan can come at you all day every day. Let's face it, we're all a walking to-do list!

DOES THIS SCENARIO SOUND FAMILIAR?

Monday morning:	You find out your psychology midterm is next Wednesday.
Monday evening:	Your mom asks if you've purchased your plane ticket to come home for fall break.
Tuesday midday:	You look at your English lit syllabus and see that the book discussion on *Wuthering Heights*, which you're only halfway through, is due on Friday.
Wednesday morning:	You realize you put on your last pair of clean underwear. You get in your car to drive to campus, and your *Check Engine* light is on. You arrive at campus, and as you're walking to your first class, your fraternity buddy yells from across the parking lot, "Hey, don't forget—you're on snack duty for tonight's meeting!" Your calculus professor reminds you about the problem set due on Friday. And as you're heading to lunch, your friend from design class asks, "When are you in studio?" and you realize you need to schedule time to work on your project.

Your brain is moving a mile a minute trying to process it all. You've got a ton to do. Where the heck do you start? How do you even remember to remember?

With a good Brain Dump! It's exactly what it sounds like—a way of getting all of those to-dos that are ping-ponging around your head out of your brain so you can more effectively and efficiently create a plan to actually do them. By doing so, you free up space in your brain, alleviating the stress of trying to remember all of the things you dumped. And by putting to-dos to paper, you can visualize them, which makes ordering, prioritizing and planning that much easier.

Do you need to do it every day? Yes. Will it hurt? Yes, until you get used to it!

Step 1: Just list your to-dos as they pop into your head. Don't think too much. The point is to just clear your head and not to focus on order or priority.

Here's what the Brain Dump from the scenario above looks like:

Psychology midterm Wednesday
Plane ticket
Wuthering Heights book
Laundry
Calculus set Fri
Design studio
Check Engine light
Frat food TONIGHT

Step 2: Make your to-dos actionable. The key here is to create some movement! It's a simple trick I use to get those mundane to-dos to literally jump off the page.

Here's what I mean:

Instead of "Plane ticket"	try "Book airline ticket."
Instead of "Design studio"	try "Schedule design studio time."
Instead of "Frat food tonight"	try "Order pizza from Uber Eats."

And a tip within a tip? Group like with like. Want to avoid an overloaded, to-do list meltdown and save time? Here's the catch: your tasks need to match. When creating your dump, put all your errands together, assignments together and emails together. My students say this trick really helps them manage their time more effectively.

WHAT'S YOUR PRIORITY?

Asking yourself "What is my priority today?" is much more effective than asking "What do I need to do today?" in terms of decision-making, sequencing and determining what is essential for you to get started on immediately.

It's not enough just to know what's on the menu. You need to know which dish you're going to order first. Otherwise, you're literally going to bite off more than you can chew.

If you tend to miss deadlines and have trouble finishing important things, start with the tasks that are most important and due the soonest. Then work on the less important stuff or things that have a longer deadline. Group your list by what you can get done now (or what we call in my house "your one-offs"), such as making the car repair appointment, separately from what needs to get done soon and needs a significant time block, such as reading *Wuthering Heights*.

Brain dumping and prioritizing are priorities in my book! You need to visualize it to plan it. And you need to plan it to achieve it.

And to achieve it, you need to schedule it.

The Digital Download
MyHomework Student Planner
A ton of electronic planner apps are out there that will have you organized and planned in no time. But I find most to be clunky or hard to use. Granted, I'm not very tech savvy, so you know if I can figure out an app and find it intuitive and easy to use, then it has to be! The myHomework Student Planner gives you a calendar to use to track your assignments, exams and other important dates, as well as a homework widget where you can sync your assignments and receive reminders for when they are due. Perfect for remembering those dreadful deadlines.

USING AN ACADEMIC PLANNER

I can hear your grunts and groans from way over here. And all the excuses as to why a planner doesn't work for you. And how much effort it takes to use. And that you don't need to use one because all your assignments are online. And even better, that you remember it all without having to write anything down.

Did I miss anything?

I feel I've been pretty flexible with my advice throughout this book. Meaning, I'm 100 percent on the YOU-figure-out-the-best-systems-and-strategies-to-help-you-stop-procrastinating-and-get-stuff-done bandwagon. But when it comes to using a planner? Nonnegotiable, as far as I'm concerned.

To-Dos

NOW	LATER	EVENTUALLY
Call Mom	Make dentist appt	Call Grandma
	Book trip home	Yogurt (Trader Joe's)

I'm constantly adding things to each section and moving items around. Because I'm checking this every day, my eventually items are always becoming laters, and my laters become nows.

So that's how I keep track of everything. But you're probably wondering, or at least my mom is, "How do you actually REMEMBER to do what's on your list?!" Well, Mom, every few days I cross-check my to-do list with my calendar to see what I can get done during the day. For me, I'm finding blocks between my meeting and call schedule, but it works the same for classes and club meetings. I take a look at my now and later sections and set reminders throughout the week based on free time in my schedule. Do I need to call the doctor? Great! I'll get that done at 11:15 on Tuesday, right after I'm done with my meeting. I set a reminder and then boom, done.

You need to use some type of planning tool to . . . well . . . plan! It's all well and good to know what you have to do and the order in which to do it (see our list on the previous pages), but a proper academic planner helps you also visualize what's ahead so you can plan (there's that word again) for and manage WHEN YOU HAVE TIME TO DO IT.

There really is no other way.

But not every planner is created equal. Most planners, especially the ones from your schools or found in campus bookstores, are formatted as to-do lists and don't allow you to see your school, after-school, evening and weekend lives as a whole. They just give you a place to record assignments and tests. That won't work if you want to truly plan and manage your time.

FEATURES OF THE PERFECT PLANNER

Here's what to look for when scouting for the perfect personal planner:

- It follows the school year (starts in either July or August and runs through the end of June) rather than the calendar year. Look for one called "academic planner" or "school planner."
- A customizable subject index (instead of preprinted subjects) where you write your class subjects only once. This feature will eliminate forgetfulness and frustration, which lead directly to procrastinating! The number one complaint I hear from my students is that their planners come with subjects already printed on them and that they are subjects they don't even take! So make sure YOU can write in YOUR schedule!
- An ample number of subject boxes so there's room to write all your classes. I recommend one that has at least six! Even if you have fewer classes, you can use one of the boxes for reminders or for an ongoing project such as college applications or thesis.
- And while you're at it, make sure the boxes are big enough to hold all the details of your assignments. Unfortunately, most planners don't, which forces students to either severely edit the information they write down or write illegibly, leading to massive confusion later.
- A grid system layout so you can see your week (and weekends!) at a glance. Weekly planner pages should line up with the subject index on a subject-by-subject basis, creating an easy method for you to record and review your weekly schedules. The bottom line? You need to see your week as a whole. So the planners that have Monday through Wednesday on one side and the remainder of the week on the other just don't cut it.
- Days of the week listed horizontally across the planner. This makes recording entries simple and allows you to see assignments and due dates and creates continuity critical for developing time management skills.
- Space to enter after-school activities and weekend commitments.

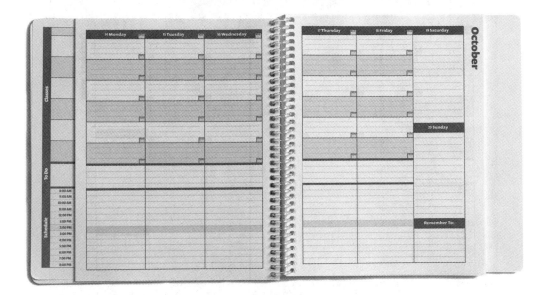

- **THIS IS WHERE THE MAGIC HAPPENS!**
  Once you enter all your activities and commitments, scheduled and available blocks of time will naturally appear. You can use those available blocks to plan your weekly workload!

  THIS IS THE KEY INGREDIENT TO PLANNING EFFECTIVELY!

- Monthly calendar views for long-range planning as well as recording vacation and school holidays. And an ample note section will help you track both personal and school to-dos.

Classroom Confessionals
Biggest "Oh, Shit" Moment?
"Thinking my test was the Wednesday after spring break and finding out it was actually the Monday we got back!"
—Alex C., college junior

OUT OF THE MOUTH OF (MY OTHER) BABE . . .

Hi. I'm Eli. I'm the son. I promised my mom (the author of this here book) that I would do this, so here we are.

I was tasked with listing my top five pieces of advice regarding procrastination that Leslie has given me through my years, as well as discussing how effective the advice has been . . . or not. She's super honest! However, to be perfectly candid, I wasn't able to do that. Just about everything I was taught regarding procrastination has been so ingrained into my lifestyle and how I function generally that I wasn't really able to identify whether or not I had been taught them or just did them instinctively. I'm not lazy, I promise you. I actually did put thought into this.

However, I will say that the absolute most important and effective piece of advice she's given me is to write things down in a planner. NO, THIS IS NOT AN ATTEMPT TO HELP SELL THEM. I'm not a sellout. But seriously, it works. And it works well. I say to you, dear reader, this is the absolute must when it comes to breaking your procrastinating ways. Keep a planner, one that shows your whole week at a glance, and put just about any assignment, event, or significant goings-on in there. Sure, it seems meticulous at first, but once you get over that, it becomes second nature, and you begin to notice that you have a much greater handle over your own time and time management as a whole. My mother knows her shit.

PAPER PLANNER POINTERS

Along with choosing the proper planner, I want to also make sure you get the optimum output from it! Here are a few planner pointers:

- List all your subjects in the index in a way that makes sense to you. Some of my students list alphabetically. Most prefer listing them in order of their day.

- If you have room, include a row in the planner for **ORGANIZING** so you can plan backpack and binder clean-outs, as well as updates to your schedule. Maintenance is the key to staying on track and feeling that you have it all under control.
- Immediately record all after-school activities, weekend commitments, parties at the sorority house, club soccer games, job hours and so on, so you can see your available blocks of time.
- Scope out that syllabus! Transfer all exam dates, group project meetings, professors' office hours and even the scheduled day and time to submit your weekly problem set in economics to your planner.
- All long-term assignments and exams should be written down in every class, **BOTH** on the day assigned **AND** on the day they are due. **PRO TIP:** Some of my students write important assignments **VERTICALLY** for due dates to truly stand out.
- Write **NO HOMEWORK** if none was assigned to ensure you haven't forgotten to record an assignment. The last thing we want is for you to forget what it is you need (or don't need) to be doing! Procrastination averted!

USING A PAPER PLANNER VS ELECTRONIC CALENDAR

This is a tough call.

I tend to favor paper planners for my students because writing information down helps us to commit it to memory better than typing. Maybe it's because writing creates better pathways in the brain to absorb information. Or maybe we instinctively attach significance to something we create that is uniquely our own. Something in our handwriting is more important than something in an impersonal font. Whatever it is, writing works!

But not all of you want or like a paper planner. If that's the case, then find an electronic version that is organized for BOTH weekly

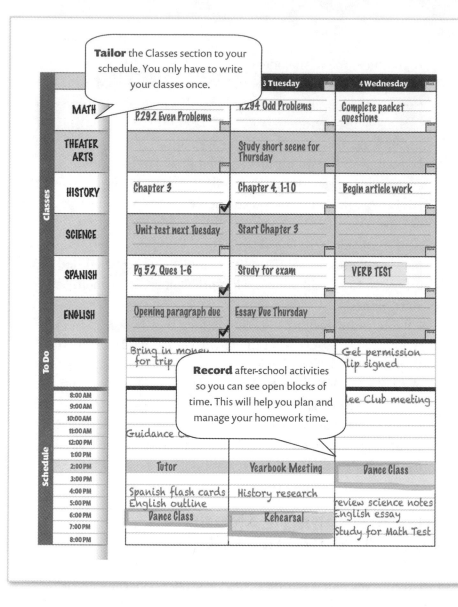

and monthly views. This gives you the big picture, the sum of all the moving parts. While electronic planners are not my favorite tools to develop true time management and planning skills, you need to start somewhere.

I would prefer you get into the habit of using an electronic device than not using anything at all.

And for those of you who refuse to use anything? Or tell me that

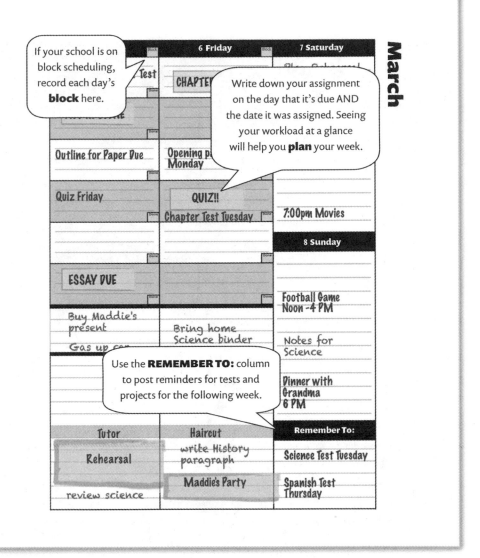

since all your assignments are on the school website you don't need to write anything down?

One professor I know actually included a planner on her supply list and made it a mandatory requirement for her college class to stress its importance. She even went so far as to predict that those students who refused to use one would fail her course.

She was right.

PAPER PLANNING: THE COMEBACK KID

I'm a paper planner girl. Always have been. Always will be. There's something about putting pen to paper that makes me feel organized, time managed and, yes, in control. And it seems I'm not the only one. In our high-tech world, paper planners are making a comeback—and in a really big way.

According to the survey done as part of the Paper and Packaging Board's recent annual back-to-school report, 63 percent of K–12 teachers' courses involved paper-based learning and that included using a student planner! The 2018 report found that 94 percent of college students and 89 percent of students in grades 7 through 12 say that paper is essential to helping them achieve their academic goals.

Want even more proof? In 2017 the *London School of Economics* recognized paper's unique role in the lives of our Gen Z students, born from the mid-1990s to early 2000s, who have grown up in a world of cell phones, laptops and touch screens. In a study of college students in ten countries, researchers found that these students still choose paper to study, read, share and send.

So when schools are posting assignments online and giving students iPads to use, why are some of you reaching for a hard-copy paper planner?

- **Writing in a paper planner helps you remember.** Philosopher and psychologist Nicolas Clausen said it best: "Typing only activates the 'language' areas of our brain; whereas writing with a pen/pencil activates multiple brain regions and therefore makes the process complex, sensory-rich and memorable." Plenty of research shows that students who take notes by hand have a higher retention rate than those who take notes on laptops.

- **Paper planners are more time efficient.** I've been selling this concept to my students for years. But it's true. How do I know? I actually test it by timing my students! I ask them to record the same homework assignment in their academic planners and then again on an electronic device. The physical planner wins every time!
- **Electronic devices are distracting!** I hear all day long that when you go to open up an app on your phone or computer to write something down, Instagram/Snapchat/text messaging/YouTube (should I go on?) starts calling your name. And of course what you intended to do never gets done.
- **Paper planners build time management skills.** I can't say this enough! They allow you to see the big picture using clear weekly and monthly views to help you create a time sense and future awareness. I can't count how many times I have heard a student say, "I need to see everything all in the same place." Seeing helps us plan, prioritize and stay on task and track.

So if you thought that paper planning was a thing of the past, well, maybe. But I think the better point is that it's very much the present and the wave of the future!

JEREMY'S STORY

Have I told you the story of my student Jeremy who carried around a roll of paper towels for his entire junior year? Now you're interested! He didn't want to use a planner or write in an electronic calendar. In his mind, there was no need. He had it all in his head. And no convincing on my part was going to persuade him otherwise.

Until one day, sitting across the kitchen table from him, I noticed that during our sessions he would rip off a paper towel from its roll and doodle on it. I asked him why paper towels rather than "real" paper or sticky notes. He didn't give me a profound answer. He just said he found it funny and provocative. And if it was funny, and then it was fun to do. Crazily enough, that made sense!

And then . . . Bingo! Something hit me. I asked Jeremy, "What if you wrote your assignments each day on a paper towel?"

I was met first with a blank stare. Then he kind of sheepishly said, "I can do that?"

"Of course you can," I told him. "I don't care how you keep track of what you need to do, as long as you do it."

Here's what I learned from working with Jeremy. Getting him to use a planner was really a two-step process. And since using a planner was the SECOND step, I needed to focus on the first—getting Jeremy to write things down. By first finding a Brain Dump tool that worked for Jeremy, we were eventually able to move on and find him a planning tool he committed to using.

PLANNING GUIDELINES FOR LONG-TERM PROJECTS AND PAPERS

Nothing gets your procrastination blood pressure rising faster than trying to tackle a long-term project or paper. Not only might it be difficult academically, but keeping track of all the steps involved and the amount of time it will take can be a time management nightmare!

| Project name: _____ | Due date: _____ |

WHAT DO YOU NEED TO ANSWER?

Thesis/questions: _____
_____
_____
_____

WHAT CRITERIA ARE REQUIRED (E.G., NUMBER OF PAGES, TYPES OF SOURCES, STYLE, FONT, ETC.)?

Guidelines: _____
_____
_____
_____

WHAT STEPS ARE NEEDED TO COMPLETE THE PROJECT?

#	Steps	Set deadline

DON'T FORGET TO ENTER YOUR DATES IN YOUR PLANNER.

WHAT TOOLS ARE NEEDED?

Materials:	
Information:	
Resources:	

Never mind a procrastination one! So you keep pushing it OFF and pushing it OFF, until you have no other choice than to flip that pesky switch ON!

I've got you covered. Use the Project Planning Guide included on the previous page while following the steps in this chapter or feel free to create one of your own.

MAKE AN OUTLINE OF THE STEPS NECESSARY TO COMPLETE THE ASSIGNMENT.

For written reports, the steps might look something like this:

Read rubric
Pick topic
Create thesis
Select sources
Search web/trip to library
Take notes
Make outline
Craft introduction
Write sections of paper (not necessarily in order)
Prepare bibliography
Create supporting documents
Proofread
Prepare final draft

BREAK LARGE PARTS OF THE ASSIGNMENT INTO SMALL ACTIONABLE TASKS.

I can't stress this point enough. Breaking things down into manageable parts makes working through them less overwhelming, which cuts down the procrastination. AND it provides multiple opportunities to enjoy the success that comes from finishing each part. Make sure each task is manageable and specific. After all, it's easier to write one paragraph every afternoon than it is to complete the entire research paper in one night.

ESTIMATE HOW MUCH TIME IT'S GOING TO TAKE YOU TO DO EACH STEP.

Work backward from the due date to figure out how much time you will need to accomplish each task. Always build in extra padding. I normally tack on an extra 25 percent to act as a buffer against false starts, interruptions and unanticipated problems.

ASSIGN DEADLINES AND SCHEDULE APPOINTMENTS FOR EACH TASK.

Assign due dates for completing each step, and record them in your planner. Remember to schedule them as regular assignments so you know exactly when you have time to work on them. This step is critical. Most of you know how to complete homework that is due the next day. However, while making time for long-term assignments and projects that can be more challenging, it is essential for crushing procrastination. Plan to finish two days in advance of the due date.

ALLOT TIME FOR HIDDEN TASKS.

The devil is in the details, my friends! Purchasing materials, visiting a museum or watching a movie, getting together with your group and proofreading drafts are all steps that are easily overlooked when factoring your time.

ARE YOU ON TRACK?

Let's be real. Even the best-laid plans go off the rails. That's why I always suggest you plan days to get them back on! As you are entering your tasks into your planner, add a few are-you-on-track days (three to four days apart) when you don't schedule any actual work but leave yourself a check-in to make sure you are on target. If you're not, then this is the time to get caught up. And if you are? Consider it a "get out of jail free" card!

FREE PERIODS ARE GIFTS. PERIOD!

Use your free periods, study halls or time between classes to work on these projects. Using downtime during school breaks or conference days to get a jump start on your assignments and projects is a great way to take the pressure off.

STUDY PLANNING VS STUDY CRAMMING

Studying for exams, especially midterms and finals, is a juggling act. And more often than not, you drop the balls!

Need more convincing? Let's play out a scenario. You have an exam on Thursday. You didn't write it down and pushed it out of your mind. Then on Wednesday night something jogged your memory. Maybe a friend asked you for help or your roommate was studying for his exams. You have your big "Oh, shit" moment! But you don't have enough time to study because your workload for Thursday is huge and you're scrambling just to finish that up. You blame your stressed-out, pit-in-the-stomach, I-feel-like-throwing-up feeling on not having enough time in your schedule. But you're wrong, my friend. The real blame lies in the fact that you didn't make a plan!

In this section, I'm going to show you the EXACT methods I teach my students for planning for a single exam and for multiple exams at once, such as midterms and finals. Most of the how-tos for studying were covered in our study skills chapter. Here, we're going to focus specifically on setting up the plan to achieve those steps.

PLANNING FOR A SINGLE EXAM

I start all my planning sessions using 8½ by 11 unlined paper OR my preprinted Study Planning Guide. Using paper allows you to SEE the whole picture easily. For this example, I'm going to use plain paper.

STUDY PLANNING GUIDE

Exam: _____ Date: _____

WHAT TOPICS ARE COVERED?

1.	4.
2.	5.
3.	6.

WHAT STUDY MATERIALS DO YOU ALREADY HAVE?

(old exams, homework, etc.)

1.	4.
2.	5.
3.	6.

WHAT TOOLS DO YOU NEED TO MAKE?

(flash cards, study guide, etc.)

1.	3.
2.	4.

M	T	W	TH	F	S	S

M	T	W	TH	F	S	S

* Don't forget to work backward
from your exam date.

* Check your planner
for unavailable times!

* Don't forget to enter
your plan in your planner!

1. **Create a three-week calendar using unlined paper.**

   Enter your exam on the designated day.

   Begin marking off days and afternoons you are unable to study. This allows you to see your available time in relation to everything else you might already have planned.

   Put in the days and times of your study groups, review sessions and so on.

2. **Define what topics will be covered.** For example, "Study for social studies test" is too big and vague. Writing "study for Mesopotamia test" is too.

   Answer the question, "What will my test specifically cover?"

   You answers might include:

   the seven gods

   inventions

   architecture

   If using the Study Planning Guide, enter the topics in the section marked "What topics are covered?" If not, write them in your notebook.

MON	TUES	WED	THUR	FR	SAT	SUN
1	2	3	4	5	6	7
8	9	10 7pm: study group	11	12 SOCIAL STUDIES TEST	13	14
15	16	17	18	19	20	21

3. **Take stock of your study tools.** Ask yourself the following questions:

   What tools do I need to use?

   What do I already have?

What do I need to create?

Your answers might include:

What tools do I need to use?	Flash cards. Videos. Study group.
What do I already have?	Old homework. Teacher's study guide.
What do I need to create?	Flash cards

Write your answers in your notebook.

4. **Assign specific tasks to each day and enter them on your calendar.**

   Monday: Create flash cards.

   Tuesday: Self-test. Pull out old exams. Answer questions in the back of the textbook. Redo old homework.

   Wednesday: Learn material you didn't know well. Use flash cards. Watch videos. Answer study guide questions. Go to study group.

   Thursday: Take sample test. Review ALL material.

MON	TUES	WED	THUR	FR	SAT	SUN
1	2	3	4	5	6	7
8 Create flash cards	9 Self Test	10 Watch Videos Go over study guide 7pm: study group	11 Take Sample Test Review Material	12 SOCIAL STUDIES TEST	13	14
15	16	17	18	19	20	21

5. **Start studying at least three days before.** This gives you extra padding in case the unexpected rears its ugly head.

   What happens if you don't have time on Tuesday but a lot of time on Monday? By planning your study schedule, creating a visual calendar and seeing your time in relation to everything else you have, you can make the necessary adjustments. Double up your time on Monday if Tuesday is jam-packed.

6. **Transfer your study plan to your planner.**

PLANNING FOR MIDTERMS AND FINALS

To plan for midterms and finals, there are a few extra steps to follow.

1. **Create a three-week calendar using unlined paper.**
    Enter your exams on the designated days.
    Assign each subject a different color.
    Begin marking off days and afternoons you are unable to study.
    Add any review sessions and group meetings that are already planned.
    Again, use a different color for each subject.**

MON	TUES	WED	THUR	FR	SAT	SUN
1	2	3	4	5	6	7
8	9 Spanish Review	10	11 Spanish Review	12 English Review / Spanish Final	13	14 English Group
15 English Final	16 Math Review	17 Science Group	18 Science Final	19 Math Final	20	21

2. **Follow steps 2 and 3 of "planning for a single exam."** (What topics are covered? What study materials do you already have? What tools do you need to make?) for each of your exams.
3. **Determine how much time you need to study for each subject.** Which subjects do you feel confident in? Which will need more of your time? Is one exam cumulative while another will cover material from the beginning of the year? Take all these factors into account.
4. **Begin assigning your subject blocks to each day.** There are a few rules of thumb to follow:

Try to study two or three subjects a day. Alternating among a few will help your brain stay fresh and active. Only schedule two-hour study blocks at a time.

A study group or teacher review session can be considered a study block. WIN!

MON	TUES	WED	THUR	FR	SAT	SUN
1	2	3	4	5	6 English Math Science SPANISH	7
8 English Math Science SPANISH	9 English SPANISH REVIEW Science	10 Math Science SPANISH	11 English SPANISH REVIEW SPANISH	12 Spanish English Review SPANISH FINAL	13	14 Science English Group English
15 Math English English Final	16 Math Review Science	17 Math Science Group Science	18 Math Science ↓ Science Final	19 Math ↓ Math Final	20	21

** Use either Sharpies or colored sticky notes. The sticky notes allow you the flexibility of moving your study blocks around until you determine the optimum plan.

5. **Once you have all your study blocks assigned, review your plan.** What do you see? Have you scheduled too much time for one subject and not enough for another? Using color to plan gives you a clear and intuitive method for seeing how much time you have allotted for each subject.
6. **Your first day of your study plan should be spent getting set up and creating the study tools you need.**
7. **Repeat step 4 under "planning for a single exam."**
8. **Transfer your study plan to your planner.**

Now you're ready to plan, no matter what comes your way!

Chapter 5
"I'LL REMEMBER"

ROUTINES AND RITUALS

The focus of this chapter is different from the other chapters in this book. That's because planning, time management and organization all require ongoing, conscious, active brainpower. Routines, almost by definition, do not. Think of a routine as "I plan it once and I'm done." It's the ability to move through your tasks without thinking about what's next. Routines are great tools to battle procrastination, because giving your brain a break from consciously planning and preparing certain to-dos means fewer things will get in your way of accomplishing the work that requires effort.

Don't just take my word for it. Mark Zuckerberg has said that he wears the same color T-shirt and hoodie every single day so he can focus his mind and energy on his work. Wearing the same outfit every day may be taking things to the extreme—couldn't he have found a more fashionable way to take this approach?—but fashion choices aside, his point makes sense. Routines can make life easier, save you time and provide a sense of calm and control.

A funny thing about routines and rituals is that sometimes they naturally form without deliberately thinking about them. Brushing your teeth before you wash your face (or after) is a routine you probably just fell into one day. The same thing with whether you put both socks on before your shoes or whether you do sock-shoe-sock-shoe.

Other routines take some thought and effort. Think about what happens at the beginning of every school year or semester when you receive your new schedule and have to figure out the structure of your days.

Just so we are all on the same page, I assure you that the goal of this chapter is not to give you a definitive, one-size-fits-all list of routines that you should be performing. Instead, it's intended to get you thinking about what routines and rituals you can develop that will reduce your mental effort, "create time" by saving time, and help break your procrastination logjam.

ROUTINE, RITUAL, REPEAT

You might be asking, "What's the difference between a routine and a ritual? Aren't they the same?" For our purpose, a routine is something you perform in a specific period of time that can be added to your planner or calendar. A ritual is an order or procedure to be followed in working (or preparing to work) on a task or activity.

Doing laundry every Tuesday night at 7:00 is a routine. But preparing yourself to begin homework each night by first getting a snack, then sitting down at your desk to organize it, turning on your lamp, firing up your playlist and finally gathering the materials you need for the assignment is a ritual.

While those examples may make them sound very different, routines and rituals are both amazing tools to fight procrastination. The best way to show you how effective they are is to show you what could happen without them in place.

The Digital Download
The Habit Hub
When you make a habit out of something, it becomes routine. The Habit Hub encourages you to create a daily habit by reminding you to perform a task and tracking when you complete it. The app creates a visual "chain" showing each day the task was completed. As the chain gets longer, it serves as an incentive to keep at the task, so you don't break the chain. You can organize your tasks into categories and then customize each one according to how often you're supposed to do it. It's incredibly flexible and makes setting up and staying in a routine a breeze.

LOSING TIME TO THE RINSE CYCLE

Let's say you don't have a set schedule for laundry. It's 8:30 on Monday night and you're about to dive into your calculus problem set. You have twelve problems and estimate it will take about an hour, leaving you enough time to read a chapter of American history afterward. As you reach for your textbook, you catch a glimpse of your laundry basket and see a shirt that you love. And you say, "I want to wear that tomorrow." So you decide to put your laundry up before you even consider whether you can do both at the same time. Can you?

Here's what you're not anticipating:

8:30	It takes you fifteen minutes to start your laundry.
8:45	You start your calculus problem set.
9:25	The buzzer on the washing machine goes off. You complete the problem you're working on (number seven) and move the laundry to the dryer.
9:40	You sit back down to continue calculus. The last five problems are very difficult, and take thirty-five minutes to finish.
10:15	You move on to your history reading but take a break to retrieve your laundry and get a snack.
11:30	You finally finish your homework. But wait! There's more! You still need to fold your laundry and prepare for the next day.
12:30	You finish everything up and go to bed—an hour later than planned.
6:00	You wake up a half hour earlier than normal to meet your science project group.

To add insult to injury, you only got seven of the twelve calculus problems correct. This homework problem set was worth 20 percent of your grade, so it drags your average down.

Doing your laundry seemed innocent enough, right? But it had unexpected consequences. One small decision threw your evening completely off course, and the ripple effect continued into the next day.

Next, let's take a look at how things would have gone differently that Monday night if you had a "Tuesday Night at 7:00 Laundry" routine.

8:30	You start your calculus problem set.
9:45	Math completed. (It took longer than the hour you estimated.)
	You take a quick dessert break and tackle your American history reading next.
11:00	You finish reading.
11:30	You go to bed, having quickly finished getting ready for the next day.
6:00	You wake up a half hour earlier than normal (but still feel rested) to meet your science project group.

Good news! You got nine of your twelve calculus problems right because you built up momentum working straight through without interruption.

And your favorite shirt, which you noticed in your hamper last night, will be ready tomorrow because tonight is laundry night! And because of that, you can structure your work around your laundry.

Which night would you rather have?

WHAT DO DIFFERENT ROUTINES LOOK LIKE?

Any task or recurring activity that you have the ability to schedule can be turned into a routine. Let's look at the example below:

ALEX'S STORY

My student Alex schedules several types of routines to help his weeks run smoothly and to procrastinate less. His routines consist of weekly and daily prep routines, study routines and life routines.

Weekly and Daily Prep Routine

Alex sets aside time in advance to prepare for both the week ahead and for the next school day. He blocks 10 p.m. Monday through Thursday to begin preparing for the next day and Sunday at 9 p.m. for his weekly prep. He sets his phone alarm for easy reminders.

MON	TUES	WED	THUR	FR	SAT	SUN
1	2	3	4	5	6	7
					10am: Gym	
	3pm: Study (Arch)	**3pm:** Gym	**3pm:** Study Time			
						5pm: Gym
						9pm: Weekly Prep
10pm: Daily Prep	**10pm:** Daily Prep	**10pm:** Daily Prep	**10pm:** Daily Prep			

Alex's daily prep includes the following:
Reviewing school and after-school schedule for the next day
Gathering everything he needs to bring to school
Making a to-do list of nonschool items
Checking wallet for cash
Charging phone
Packing backpack
Making lunch
Leaving everything by the front door

Alex's weekly prep includes the following:
Reviewing his schedule and assignments for the week ahead
Making notes and blocking out times for other weekly routines
Creating a weekly to-do list of nonschool items
Calculating and planning for travel time for any activities
Informing his parents of changes or unusual times in his schedule
    (late-night rehearsals, early-morning meetings)

As Alex learned, setting these prep times provides double benefits. After a while, his 10 p.m. prep not only became a nightly routine he stopped thinking twice about, but his days flowed more easily because his tasks, activities and other to-dos were already scheduled, packed and planned for.

Study Routines

During Alex's weekly and daily prep time, he made sure to plan his study time. I know, it sounds kind of obvious, right? But Alex doesn't just set aside time to study. He takes it one step further and creates a Tuesday afternoon after-school routine of working on his final archaeology project.

By doing so, he knows that when Tuesday at three rolls around, it's time to focus on that project and that project only. He doesn't think about juggling his schedule to make time for it. And since the time is dedicated to the project, no other work will get in the way. Deciding what to do as that time rolled around would be confusing or overwhelming at best and procrastinating at worst.

LIFE ROUTINES

Here's a little paradox: the time, effort and energy spent thinking about doing activities that have nothing to do with schoolwork can be a major source of procrastination.

But many of these activities, such as exercise and self-care, are super productive and support your mental and physical well-being. And being in a good place both mentally and physically is one of the best defenders against procrastination. If we take a look at Alex's schedule again, we see that he schedules his gym time, giving it the same prominence and importance as his other commitments.

WORKOUTS, SELF-CARE AND MORNINGS

What can you do to preserve and promote the benefits of nonschool activities while jettisoning those aspects of them that get in your way?

PLAN YOUR WORKOUTS

Workout Wednesday. When figuring out a routine, make sure to take into account your other commitments. Be realistic in your choosing. If you're not a morning person, is a 7 a.m. spin class really going to happen?

Block it out. By scheduling ahead of time, you avoid staring at both a laundry list of competing to-dos AND the desire to work out. That type of decision-making dilemma directly leads to procrastination and sometimes . . . doing nothing!

Go next door. Is your psych class in the building next to the campus gym? You might not have thought of this, but you already have part of a routine in place! Going to the gym after class may mean you have to forgo meeting your friends for lunch on that day, but it's always easier to put a routine in place or stick to one when what you need to do is right there!

Treat exercise like an appointment. By designating your workout times as appointments, you avoid scheduling something else in their place. Protecting your time will ensure it gets done.

Have clothing you need on hand. Keep your exercise gear in your backpack so you are never without. I have a student who sleeps in hers so she can kick it into gear right when she wakes up.

SCHEDULING SELF-CARE

With your life filled to the brim with school, jobs, activities, friends, family and more, it is essential that you set up a self-care routine. Self-care can take on many forms, such as a long shower, a bath, a power nap, reading a book, taking a walk or chatting with a friend. Anything that makes you feel recharged and refreshed mentally. And by scheduling your self-care time and making it a routine, you reduce the urge to use time better spent working and being productive.

BOOKEND YOUR DAYS

This is for all my college kids out there! When my students are picking their classes for a new semester, I have them try to "bookend" their days as much as possible. What does that mean?

When you're in high school, it's easy to have a consistent routine. You get up at the same time, go to school at the same time, have class at the same time. You get the picture. College throws that all off. One morning you start at nine, another day not until one! Nothing derails a routine more than planning to get up at eight for some serious library time only to sleep until noon! Epic fail!

So my students try to schedule their classes to begin and end at the same time every day. Not an easy task and not always in their control. If that's impossible, we set the morning routine so that they get up at the same time every day. They find this critical in establishing productive and consistent routines. And for starting their mornings off stress-free! Bonus!

MORNINGS

A lot of folks think mornings are easy. Get up. Shower. Dress. Eat breakfast. Out the door.

For others, each morning is the beginning of another day of mental, emotional and physical quicksand.

Morning rituals set the tone for the day. If your morning goes smoothly and effortlessly, it's a lot easier to tackle the rest of your day. But if you are harried and aggravated and very late when you walk out of your house or dorm or apartment, you'll likely carry those feelings into your first class.

Here are some helpful tips to set your morning routine on the right track:

Order your activities. There's no right or wrong order to do things in the morning. But to create an efficient morning ritual, you should think about how you move from one morning activity to the next and try to make those transitions as smooth as possible.

Pick your clothes for the next day. Do you know how much time is eaten up by playing the "shirt and switch"? If you're the kind of person who might be tempted to change things up in the morning (which would waste the time you thought you saved by picking your outfit the night before), take the clothes out of your bedroom and put them in or near the bathroom. Any place that is away from your bedroom! Or create a clothing rotation. That could mean picking a different outfit or a different style for each day of the week.

Prepare breakfast the night before. If you live at home or in an off-campus apartment, a lot of time can get lost trying to figure out what you're going to have for breakfast. Get into a routine of setting up the coffee for your morning brew. Get out utensils, pour your cereal, have eggs ready. You will shave minutes off your morning and ensure a smooth and healthy one to boost!

Set up a launching pad. Getting showered, dressed, fed and out the door efficiently is all well and good—until you discover that you left your notebook with your assignment sitting on your desk. Or your wallet. Or your (fill in the blank).

My favorite fix is a *launching pad*! It's a designated place in your home or dorm where you keep the belongings that go back and forth to school or class. A launching pad takes the stress of packing for the day out of the equation. Pick a trafficked area that you pass by regularly—and definitely pass on your way out the door in the morning—like near the front door or right outside your room. Backpacks, completed homework, books, gym clothes, even glasses and wallets can all be stored here.

And a tip within a tip? Some of my students have a charging station in their launching pad so they can just grab their electronics and go in the morning!

Go to bed! If you follow all these tips and still struggle in the morning, there's one last "night before" item you should consider—a good night's sleep! You're not going to be able to function effectively if you're exhausted. So shut off Netflix, step away from Snapchat Stories and set a bedtime. You'll thank yourself in the morning.

RITUALS

Remember that ritual I mentioned a few pages back? The one where you get a snack, sit at your desk, organize it, turn on your lamp, fire up your playlist and gather your materials for your assignment?

That's six separate actions to take before you start working, only two of which (sitting and gathering your materials) are ABSOLUTELY NECESSARY for you to begin. Meaning you may think the other four are things you should not bother planning for. But turning those actions into a ritual actually *saves* you time and increases your productivity. Let me share Melanie's story to show you how.

Classroom Confessionals
What's something you do to study that none of your friends do?
"Take my shoes off, handwrite my typed notes to memorize things . . . nothing that weird!" —Marti, college junior

MELANIE'S STORY

Melanie, a high school senior, lamented constantly that it was very difficult for her to get a good flow going when she began her homework. As she described it, all the starts and stops were frustrating and led to her procrastinating. As part of my work, I observed her rituals and routines (or lack of them). Here's how Melanie began her homework that evening.

Melanie sat down and pulled out whatever schoolwork she wanted to start on.

Soon after, she got up to get a snack.

When she returned, she realized that since her desk was piled high with clutter, she couldn't find the note cards she had created the night before to study for her history test. Melanie stopped working and took fifteen minutes to clean and organize her workspace.

She finally got back to work for about twenty minutes . . . and then it started to get dark outside. Melanie got up again to turn on her lamp. She saw her sister's sweater sitting in the corner of her room and immediately left to return it.

See where I'm going here?

By not having a set prework ritual in place, Melanie left at least four different opportunities to interrupt herself while she was working. And each time it happened, she had to reengage and reactivate her brain, doubling the time it took her to accomplish her work. By creating a homework ritual for Melanie to follow, we eliminated those interruption opportunities and made her feel more efficient and productive, which allowed her to bust that procrastination pitfall.

Classroom Confessionals
Favorite study tool?
"Giant Post-its to write everything down." —Amanda, college junior

THE POWER OF THE PROTEIN

When do you feel the most likely to procrastinate? When you are exhausted and hungry or when you're full of energy and ready to go? Don't discount what optimizing your energy levels can do for you in fighting off the procrastination bug.

Whenever my students feel tired and need energy before sitting down to work, we use protein-rich foods as the magic elixir. I'm not a nutritionist, but I've read countless articles and heard dozens of professionals speak about how the right foods directly affect brain function. Protein and certain forms of complex carbs will give you energy, while your brain gets that much-needed boost. Sure, sugary drinks, candy and processed carbs such as potato chips and cookies will give you a burst of energy, but then you burn out quickly. Refueling with the proper food when you feel mentally drained will help you stay focused and on task. **Eating healthy should be part of your daily ROUTINE!**

Here are a few brain-boosting snacks to try:
raw nuts and dried fruits
banana smothered in peanut butter
protein smoothie with fresh fruit and almond butter
hummus with carrot sticks or celery
sunflower seeds
yogurt and granola
protein bars
jerky

WHAT IS YOUR WORK RITUAL?

Ground zero for procrastination is the time just before you actually sit down to tackle a task or to prepare your brain for deep work. If you can use that time to perform several actions that support your work and eliminate distractions, you might be able to smooth your transition into work mode and cut back on wasted time.

The brain is a muscle and it needs exercise. Working is exercising! But before you do any type of exercise, you need to warm up your muscles. So think of setting up a work ritual as warming up your brain to get it ready to do the heavy lifting! Here's a fun list of some of my students' favorite prework rituals:

gym	read	have a snack
coffee	crossword puzzle	call someone
take a walk	pray	walk the dog
shower	meditate	dance
light a candle	play an instrument	
music	write out priorities	

Which ones would you put on your list? Don't feel you need them all! Just pick two or three to do right before you start a tough task.

WHO'S ON ICE (IN CASE OF EMERGENCY)?

I'm not talking about your parents here or your frat bro who always knows where the best parties are on Saturday night! My students are required to keep a list of two people in each of their classes who they can call (or text!) if they need an accountability partner or to simply check in. Nothing gets you into gear faster than knowing you have to let your friend know what you did or didn't accomplish! A supportive friend—who you can text or email with a list of what you want to accomplish each day—can help keep you on task.

Chapter 6
"I KNOW WHERE EVERYTHING IS"

ORGANIZING

It's really difficult to talk about procrastination without mentioning organization. They go hand in hand. If you want to stop procrastinating, organize your bedroom or dorm room, study area (if you have one), and even your school supplies. Organizing these zones will help you work more efficiently and stay focused, alleviate the overwhelming feeling of living in a messy environment and avoid the exhausting mantra of "I'm looking for the book I need to read for class, and I have no idea where it is!"

Don't get nervous. I'm not going to unpack every organizing system imaginable. Since everyone learns differently, everyone organizes differently. I couldn't possibly know what works best for you. Some of you might take a "clean off my desk" approach when it comes to working, while others find having all their books and papers spread out inspiring and creativity inducing. Some of you might like color to infuse energy into your work, while others need calm, soothing surroundings to be productive.

I'm just going to give you some general rules to follow to make your school supplies more streamlined, your room more manageable and, therefore, your environment more productive.

YOUR BEDROOM
Play out this scenario. The adults in your life tell you to clean up

The Digital Download
Evernote

Evernote has been around for ages, and there is a reason for that. It's one of the best apps out there for keeping you and your assignments organized. It's like having electronic binders without all the excess weight! It's my number one recommended app for a variety of amazing reasons.

It allows you to sync notes across all your devices. So if you are working on your history paper on your laptop and then later switch to your desktop, you won't lose a thing.

You can take notes in many different formats—text, photos, audio, videos and more.

You can attach word processing documents and PDFs and share those documents with others.

And you can set reminders for yourself.

If it would just call your parents and do your laundry for you too, it would be pretty much perfect!

your room. With all good intentions you walk into your room, survey the scene, pick up an item from your floor and realize you have no idea where to begin, what to do, or where to put things. So you close the door and hope they won't notice. Until they do. And then the accusations start flying.

"You live like a slob!"

"We should hang a condemned sign on the door!"

"You never clean your room when I ask you!"

And the inevitable, *"Just one time I would love for you to stop procrastinating and just do it without my having to ask you!"*

How many times have you heard these kinds of phrases in your lifetime? About a million, I'm sure.

But here's what I want YOU to know. The constant struggle between you and your parents about your room isn't necessarily all your fault. But I'm thinking you feel it might be. When parents ask me how to get their kids to organize their rooms AND keep them that way, I lob a question right back at them.

I ask if your bedroom is set up to make it easy for you to create and maintain an organizing system. If they can't answer that, I send them on a tour. Of your room. Using YOUR height as the guide. And answering the following questions from your perspective. Go ahead and do it too.

**Can you open the closet door easily? Or is it
   partially blocked?**
Can you reach the rod and shelves?
**Are the things you need to access frequently or daily in your
   prime real estate?**
Are the dresser drawers hard to open?
Is the dresser crammed full?
Do you have enough room to store all your clothes?
**Do you have enough hangers? Hooks? Storage bins
   and boxes?**
**Do you have adequate shelf space for books, memorabilia,
   electronics, and so on?**
**Do you have a bulletin board or cork squares hanging on
   the wall?**
Trash bin? Laundry basket?
**A nightstand for a clock, extra alarm, lamp and
   water bottle?**
**Are there clothes or other items that don't belong to you
   stored in your room?**

Pretty eye-opening, huh?
But wait, I saved the best question for last.

Do you know where everything in your room goes?

The first rule when organizing is, **everything needs a home.** It's really that simple. No matter what your organizing style, if you don't know where something lives, you're more apt to let it sit wherever it lands. That partially explains the land mine that is your floor!

I'm well aware that you can't make all the changes on your own. I'm hoping you will show this section of the chapter to the grown-ups in your life and ask them to go on the tour of your room with you. Then perhaps you can all come up with solutions for the items on the list that need to be remedied.

But meanwhile, here are a few guidelines to help you get started on your own:

TEN TIPS TO A BETTER ORGANIZED BEDROOM

1. **Before you organize anything, you need to purge, toss, pitch, recycle or donate.** I don't care what you do with it as long as whatever you don't use, need or want is gone. Is your room loaded with empty water bottles, food wrappers, cords to electronics you don't own anymore? Grab a garbage bag and out it goes. Camp sweatshirts from when you were twelve? Donation pile!

   And a tip within a tip? Make it fun! Crank your favorite music and throw yourself a dance party. Set a timer and play Beat the Clock by seeing how much you can get done before it goes off! Grab your favorite snack and have a treat while you make it neat! Infusing energy and play into your organizing session is a great way to get moving!

2. **Designate specific homes for all of your belongings.** And make sure your areas are clearly labeled. That includes closet shelves and dresser drawers or bins. When you're tired after a long day, visual reminders make putting your stuff away that much easier.

3. **If you need to see your stuff so you know it exists or the closet door is a real hassle, then remove it!** A closet door is a barrier to entry. And we all know that barriers to entry lead right to

Classroom Confessionals
Favorite food to eat while studying?
"Bagel or Kit Kat."
—Alex, college junior

procrastination's door! Talk to your family about removing the closet door so you can see what's inside. If you can't bear to always look at your crowded closet, hang curtains above the opening so you can close it off at any time.

4. **If folding clothes isn't your jam, replace your dresser with clear bins lined against a wall to toss shirts, jeans, socks, underwear, and other clothing into.** This gives you an easy and simple way to get and stay organized. Detest hanging up clothes on hangers because it takes too many steps? Hang hooks on the closet rod instead. One step and done!

5. **Put your essentials in your prime real estate (between your shoulders and knees) for easy access.** If you have to reach up or move several items out of the way to put something away, then the likelihood of your doing it is super slim.

6. **Think air space.** If you have ample wall space, hang a bulletin board, cork squares or even a peg board (my favorite). They all come in fun colors, are easy to hang, and provide space for notes, papers, and anything else that is hard to organize.

7. **Clear shoe bags are a great space maximizer.** Hang them in your closet or behind your bedroom door. Store small items, cords and wires for your electronics, jewelry, socks and underwear, toiletries or any other loose items for an instant catch-all and to maximize your space. Amazing for dorm rooms!

8. **Clear is king!** If you can't see it, it doesn't exist. Transparent bins give you a natural way to see what you own and where it goes.

PAGE PROTECTING

You'll always have a few papers that you need to refer to over and over throughout the semester or year. Think chemistry's periodic table of elements or your Spanish verb chart. And how many times are they lost to sea? They're impossible to find! Sheets like these that need to be referenced regularly should be inserted into plastic page protectors and placed in the FRONT of the corresponding binder section. Think of it as a plastic life preserver!

9. **Create a designated area in your room to store your textbooks, extra supplies, resource materials and anything else that you need for school.** It doesn't matter where you do your homework. You still want to have one zone, preferably in your bedroom, as your go-to. Nothing derails a procrastinator more than spending time looking for stuff they need.

10. **Pair like with like.** I can't stress this enough. Make sure you store everything that goes together in one place. So for example, if you have a printer, keep printer paper, ink, toner and even batteries together. The fewer places you need to look for things, the more likely you will be able to find them quickly and efficiently.

YOUR SCHOOL SUPPLIES

Over the years, I've seen a staggering number of my high school students struggle with trying to manage folders, binders, spirals and more. It's overwhelming. And according to their complaints it leads to major procrastinating if they have to wade through endless supplies to find what they need to do.

Therefore, the first order of business is to simplify supplies any way you can. Less stuff to manage = greater organization. Most of you need a simple, manageable solution to organize your school papers so you spend less time on the looking and more time on the doing! Here are a few of my recommendations:

DITCH THE HOMEWORK FOLDER

These are dumping grounds where important assignments and papers go to die. I know a lot of experts don't agree with me on this, but trust me when I say I've never met a homework folder that worked. Instead, group all materials by subject. Math homework goes in the math binder. Your science lab in the science folder.

ORGANIZE WITH BINDERS

I recommend two types of organizing systems.

One organizing system that works well for my students who like to keep each subject in its own individual binder is a combination binder/pocket folder system. Each binder combines a loose-leaf section for taking notes AND a folder/file system for housing homework, tests and other loose papers. Extra bonus? This takes three-hole punching out of the equation!

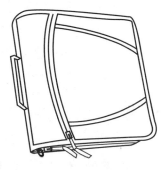

My second organizing system, for those of you who like to have everything in one place, is a master binder system. This all-in-one system houses all your subjects in tabbed sections in a zippered binder.

First, purchase a zippered binder that also contains an accordion folder. I prefer the ones that have two sets of rings, since the double rings allow you to customize the binder in a way that works for your schedule. Think "A/B" days, or morning/afternoon classes. The accordion folder is where you keep all papers, handouts, returned tests and related things. Label each section in the accordion by subject name (English, math, science and so on).

All papers will be filed BEHIND the corresponding subject tab and the most recent papers always go in the front. Schedule weekly clean-outs, as papers tend to build up quickly.

The three-ring section should be used for notes you take in class. Divide this section by subject by using two-sided translucent divider folders with tabs for each subject. Label the sides of each folder "Homework to-do" and "Homework done." This takes the guesswork out of where homework will live each night!

THE BEST SCHOOL SUPPLIES FOR COLLEGE STUDENTS

In college, your workload is at a higher level than in high school. According to my students, the right supplies and organizing system can make all the difference in your productivity and success. Here are their top five must-haves:

Folders, Folders, Folders

Surprise! College professors, TAs and advisers DO NOT HOLE PUNCH. My best advice? Make sure to have a folder for each class (preferably color-coded) so that all important papers and handouts can be stashed immediately. Keep a hole punch and binders in your dorm room to file later if you like.

Big Rings

The best way to keep notebooks and folders together is to use big metal rings, available at any office supply store. For large lecture classes, it's much easier to use a notebook and a folder in corresponding colors, held together by a ring, than to try to keep a binder under control.

Typed Notes

The transition from taking paper notes in high school to being able to use a laptop in college can trip students up. Make sure to establish a workable system, whether it is Google Docs, Evernote

The goals of a master system like this are to keep everything in one place and make finding what you need a breeze. This all-in-one system is easy to create and easy to manage.

MAINTAIN YOUR SYSTEMS

If you use any of these systems, you will have to clean them out regularly to prevent them from becoming unwieldy. A good rule is to or just plain old Word docs. Set up subject folders on your computer BEFORE THE SEMESTER BEGINS, so notes can easily be categorized, saved and accessed as needed, anywhere and at any time.

And a tip within a tip? Don't forget to back up EVERYTHING to the cloud or use an external hard drive. Trust me. A time will come when you will spill ginger ale on your computer, and you will thank me!

Notes from Advising

Designate a notebook (doesn't have to be huge) and a folder for anything handed out at academic advising meetings. Often these papers have key info and deadlines, so make sure you write any key dates in your planner before you file papers away.

Keep a small notebook in your backpack or have the Notes app handy on your phone for jotting any notes or questions specific to academic advising. When appointments with your adviser come up, these notes can make those meetings much more productive.

Desk

Magazine files are your best friend when you are short on surface space. If your dorm room desk has a hutch, place the magazine files on top, label one for each class and place all your books and folders there when not in use. This makes grab-and-go time a breeze.

empty them after a unit or chapter test or when a project or paper is completed. But what to do with all that paper?

Figure out what you can toss and then find the best way to store what you need to hold on to. Don't make it complicated. There are many creative and out-of-the-box ways to keep paper contained. Pretty bins, magazine files, binders, or even just a box will do just fine. The important thing is to make sure you maintain your system, so you don't get buried under all that excess paper.

MATT'S STORY

Years ago, I was working with Matt, a high school senior, whose parents were worried about his procrastination. They complained that it took him way too long to complete his homework. What should have taken him two hours in their estimation took him twice as long. They thought he had problems budgeting his time (Matt didn't really disagree with that assessment) and wanted me to work with him to develop his time management skills. After observing Matt, I noticed that he was highly disorganized. He never wrote down any of his assignments or remembered what was assigned. He always seemed to have trouble finding things he needed to do his work. He would spend precious time looking for lost papers and misplaced textbooks. He constantly texted his friends to ask what was due the next day. And then waited for them to text back. All of this took hours out of his designated homework time.

Was Matt procrastinating because he couldn't manage his time (as he and his parents assumed) or because he was chronically disorganized? Only after we were able to zero in on the fact that being disorganized was what was causing the procrastination were we able to brainstorm some appropriate solutions.

I worked with Matt on some much-needed organizing systems so that he could access his assignments and materials quickly and efficiently. After that, he was able to begin and finish his homework in an efficient and timely fashion.

COLOR-CODING

Do you have trouble keeping track of class assignments, your day-to-day gear and everything in between? You might want to try color-coding to make things a little easier and more streamlined. I'm a huge fan!

Color-code school supplies, designating a color for each class. Use that color for every binder, folder and notebook needed for that class. Follow the color scheme for storage bins and magazine files used for class-specific supplies. (For example, if math is red, then the calculator goes in the red bin.) To color-code your to-do list, use sticky notes in different colors to keep track of tasks like school assignments or chores. Or let the color of the sticky note convey how urgent an assignment or chore is.

Some of my students find it helpful to distinguish what they learned in class from what they learned reviewing at home. To differentiate easily, use color-coding to distinguish class notes from home-study notes—use a blue pen for class notes and a black one for home. This way, if a question comes up, at least you'll know where it originated.

Color can help you coordinate your nonschool stuff too. Organize your activity equipment by color. Use large totes in different colors—red for dance, blue for tennis, green for club soccer and so on.

Multiple devices mean lots of chargers and cords. They were always disappearing at my house until we color-coded our devices by individual (with permanent marker or a strip of colored tape on the cable). No more getting away with stealing chargers!

Classroom Confessionals
Favorite study tool?
"Take pictures on my phone of textbook pages or lecture slides and study them during random moments."
—Cole, college junior

CREATING A MOTIVATING ENVIRONMENT

Always looking internally for motivational inspiration to get something done is ineffective and exhausting! And generally leads us down the path of not getting anything accomplished. Setting up your environment so it communicates to you that it's time to get moving removes the pressure of always relying on yourself.

Let me explain.

I believe that to get motivated, people need to create positive energy around their tasks. Your environment plays a huge role in encouraging you to initiate and complete your work. If you don't like

TIPS FOR STAYING ORGANIZED DURING THE COLLEGE APPLICATION PROCESS

Some find the college search to be a massive undertaking. It's an enormous, drawn-out project with so many moving parts that it's easy for a procrastinator to go into shutdown mode.

My best advice is to treat it as you would any of your school subjects. Make "College Application" a subject in your planner. This way, you are sure to incorporate the work necessary for college applications with the rest of your studies. Here are a few more suggestions:

Use a planner or calendar. If you think you can do this without one, you're kidding yourself. You need to keep track of all application deadlines, financial aid and scholarship dates, campus visits, alumni interviews, in-school meetings with your guidance counselor and a million more things. If you need to be on top of a deadline or date, write it down.

Set up a special organizing system just for your college search. It's easy to get overwhelmed by the college mailers, supplements, essays and recommendations that take over your life during senior year. Use a milk crate or desktop filing system to make materials easily accessible, portable and visual. Create a file for each school so you can easily drop in any brochures,

where you spend your time, you're not going to get down to business, no matter what that business is.

Aim to create an environment that will make you happy and motivated so you can finish strong every time. Think of it like a caffeine boost.

I want you to open your bedroom door or head to your favorite study spot and have it send a message to you that it's time to get work done. Right now. And here's the good news: when it comes to setting up your environment so that it elicits a motivating response, **YOU** have a ton of control.

supplements or financial aid information specific to each college.

Break down your essay writing. Don't think that you're going to get all your essays or even the one for the Common Application done in one sitting. Set realistic expectations as you go. It's a lot easier to plan to write two paragraphs in one afternoon than a whole essay.

Check it off. Staple a checklist to the front of each folder that includes the school name, application due dates, and the requirements for references, essays, portfolio, financial aid and anything else. Transfer all important dates to your master calendar or planner so you stay on track.

Organize your campus visits. My daughter, Maddie, a college graduate, offers this advice: "Create an evaluation sheet to use as a Brain Dump after each visit. It will help you differentiate the information you receive from each info session and campus tour. Immediately after each visit write down your thoughts while they are still fresh in your head. It also helped to organize my notes so they would be usable when writing my supplemental essays." And bring a notebook and the school's file folder with you on your campus visit. Place any handouts you receive directly into your folder so that nothing gets lost between your visit and home. You can put the folder back into the file box when you arrive home.

Color. Color is a great way to infuse energy and fun into your space. I've never met a student who likes staring at a sea of blank, boring walls every day. So if bare is blah, then it's time to go to town and literally paint the town red. Or in your case, it might mean painting your bedroom walls orange, neon pink, striped or even zebra print. The only thing that matters is that you use your favorite color or pattern. (And that you get permission from whoever owns those walls!) If painting a room is not in the cards, then hang colorful tapestries, fabric or even removable wallpaper stickers to achieve the same effect.

COMMON APPLICATION—MAKE IT COUNT!

Print multiple copies of the Common Application and any supplements required by the colleges you are applying to. Answer all the questions FIRST in a word processing document, and then transfer your answers to the computer form. Remember, there is no going back once you hit Submit!

And a tip within a tip? Be mindful of word and character count. Some essays require a certain number of words, while others count characters.

And don't forget that rugs, furniture, throws, pillows, room accessories, picture frames and even knickknacks can all add that burst of color you crave.

Light. Situate your desk or work area near a window. Research shows that natural light increases productivity, creates less stress and improves overall health. (I'm literally sitting outside as I write this!)

And here's a fun fact. Studies also show that overhead cool-white fluorescent lighting (the kind you find in classrooms) ricochets off the surface of assignments into your eyes, a reflection that causes a type of unintended glare called veiling reflection, which interferes with your ability to read words on paper. Poor lighting reduces the effectiveness of the brain's power to gather data. Imagine bringing that excuse to your teacher or professor!

Cool tools. Some of you love the beginning of a new school year for the sole fact that you get to buy new supplies. Oh, come on. I know

Classroom Confessionals
Favorite food to eat while studying?
"Dried mango." —Casey, college sophomore

you're out there. If you have favorite pens, love pretty folders or even can't get started on a paper or project unless you have neon sticky notes or index cards by your side, then use that to your advantage. If these kinds of tools make you happy, then you'll be more productive.

Eye candy. Posters, artwork, old album covers, a collage of your hometown friends, your college banner, sports memorabilia, memorable sayings. The list goes on. Anything that promotes positive imagery and gets you to work in the space you create will do.

Noise. I know we discussed music in the homework chapter, but this is more about controlling or canceling the noise in your environment. Invest in a good pair of headphones or a white noise machine to drown out distractions. Or check out apps that give you different sounds to listen to. My favorite is rain forest sounds.

The Digital Download
StickK
When you're working alone, it's super easy to procrastinate. You don't have anybody holding you accountable and no consequences are hanging over your head. StickK to the rescue! It lets you put your money where your mouth is. Literally! You actually lose money if you don't do what you commit to doing! Here's how it works:

You set a goal and commit to doing it over a period of time. (I'm going to study for my econ test for the next five days, or I'm going to clean and organize my room every Tuesday evening.) Set a sum of money that you are willing to lose if you don't reach your goal. Make sure to pick a sum that will be painful enough to motivate you but doesn't leave you penniless if you fail. You can even invite supporters for extra accountability and a referee who confirms whether you succeed in reaching your goal.

You decide who gets your money if you fail. And here's where it has got to hurt. You want to pick a cause you don't believe in or a person you deeply dislike! Because no one wants to lose money that way!

Scent. Don't laugh. Many of my students swear by aromatherapy or even lighting candles to help them get their motivation mojo. And they're on to something! Aromatherapy is an easy and effective way to soothe the brain, improve your mood and increase your energy levels, leading to greater productivity. Try scents such as peppermint, lemon, cinnamon, eucalyptus or lavender to calm and center you.

Food. Now I'm speaking your language! There is no greater magic elixir when it comes to getting moving than when food is involved. Can you think of a time when pizza helped you out of a massive procrastination fix? Or frozen yogurt? (That's mine!) In the routines and rituals chapter we discussed which foods actually give your brain the much-needed energy boost it needs to get work done. But for now, I just want you to think about which foods I could bribe you with, so you get working.

I have a fun story to share with you about the power of popcorn. Yes, popcorn.

SAM'S STORY

Sam was a high school junior when we first met. Not only did he not like working, he also didn't like working with me. And he wasn't shy about telling me so. So, in the beginning, we didn't get very much done during our sessions. He wouldn't budge. And I was frustrated. Until one time, I asked him, for no other reason than I was trying to connect with him, what his favorite food was. He told me popcorn. So doing everything I could to get him to like me (I do that from time to time), I asked him if he wanted to go to the kitchen and make some to munch on while we had our session. He brought back a big bowl and we got started.

I quickly noticed that something had changed. Sam was more alert, willing to listen to my instructions and could keep his energy level up throughout the session. Not knowing if he was just being polite because I had suggested a fun activity, I mentioned the popcorn again at our next session. And the same results happened. Wanting to build on Sam's success, I asked Sam to do a little experiment for me when he was working alone. For the times in between our sessions, when Sam sat down to study, I wanted him to have popcorn by his side and to record the results. As you might imagine, it worked. Sam felt it was easier to do a task that he detested (studying) when it was paired with something he loved (popcorn). This perfect pairing lasted all the way through Sam's college years, and it still gets him through some critical deadlines at his job.

Chapter 7
"FIVE MORE MINUTES"

DISTRACTIONS

Can I have your attention?

Over the years the most common thread among all my students is the topic of distractions—and how to overcome them.

Distractions are everywhere, whether you're a high schooler trying to figure out how to stay focused on your homework while your younger siblings run around you or a college student adjusting to living with a roommate. And then there is the six-hundred-pound gorilla in the middle of the room, which may be better described as the one-pound digital appendage attached to your body 24-7. We're all guilty of that, including me!

But the thing about distractions—both internal and external—is they're impulsive. They catch us off guard. And when we don't plan for them, it can lead to some serious procrastinating.

In this chapter, instead of just listing all the ways you get distracted with a few helpful hints thrown in, I've pulled out a few of my students' most frequently asked questions from my time in the trenches and shared my signature solutions.

I am sure you'll see yourself in a few of them!

? HOW DO I BUST THE NETFLIX BINGE?

"My schedule this semester is jam-packed. I start my days at nine a.m. and have back-to-back classes until four p.m. It's a grueling schedule that leaves me exhausted and depleted by the end of the day. I literally have no gas in my tank when I need to start my homework. Before I start studying, I really need to take a break and unwind. My go-to is to turn on Netflix and watch what should be a quick episode of a show. It's easy and mindless and helps me get back into gear. However, it too often turns into a marathon binge session. One episode turns into three! How do I really limit myself and turn it off to get my work done?"

I get it! Days are long. Classes are exhausting. And it can be very beneficial to your productivity to take a break in between classes and homework to transition your brain.

I'll also give you the benefit of the doubt, because more often than not we don't PLAN to binge-watch anything, but streaming services make it way too easy to fall down that rabbit hole. Remind me to tell you the story of my *Stranger Things* marathon that lasted twenty-four hours. I'm not proud.

The autoplay feature on streaming platforms takes the decision-making out of watching television. How many times do you look up and not even realize that a new episode or season has begun?

So, how do we take back control?

Turn off autoplay! Streaming platforms default to this! Did you know that? I didn't until I did a bit of research, but by turning it off and having to physically select your next binge episode makes you much more aware of how long you've been watching. That reminds me of the days when I had to physically get off the couch to change the channel. Yes, it was a thing. Ask your parents.

Set a time or episode limit. It's too easy to say "five more minutes" when no boundary has been set or there is no plan in place. However, we hold ourselves much more accountable when we have to shut down by 4:30 p.m. Blocking your time helps counteract falling into the all-too-familiar black hole and busts that procrastination bug.

And a tip within a tip? This is where your timer is your best friend. Remember, setting your timer gives you a visual cue as to where you are in time.

Activate the sleep timer function. If you're thinking, "Wow, Leslie, this is great, but I'm one of the few people who still watches regular TV," or "It's too easy to click *next* on my remote and this will never work," don't worry! There's a solution to that too! Buried deep in the settings of your TV is a handy sleep timer function. Just choose how long you plan to watch and unwind—**within reason**—and when that time comes, the TV shuts off, forcing you back to your work. Procrastination gone!

? HOW CAN I STOP THE SURF?

"So much of my schoolwork is done on my computer. Not only do I use it for the day-to-day work, I also need it to reference my assignments on my class home pages, download my professors' slideshows, conduct research, watch instructional videos and search for answers to homework questions. And of course, I find myself scrolling endlessly on Instagram or browsing online shopping sites instead of doing what I need to. I've tried turning off the Wi-Fi, but that only works when I'm writing a paper. How can I continue working on my laptop without sliding down that slippery procrastination slope?"

This might be **the most common** way that my students get distracted. And guess what? I don't blame them. Our computers hold (almost) our entire lives, and I'd be lying if I said I haven't found myself browsing online when I'm "taking a quick break" from responding to emails. But there are a few ways computers make it easy for us to hide distractions and clean up our desktops.

Each subject lives alone. In the same way you put different subjects' assignments at different stations around a table or room (see the homework chapter), you should do the same with your internet browser windows. Writing a research paper? Dedicate one browser

The Digital Download
Offtime

Sometimes we all need a little app help to ignore all those calls, notifications and text messages that bombard us. Offtime allows you to temporarily disable all the distracting apps, messages and calls! Just set the time period for when you want to work. It blocks all interruptions on our phones and makes it impossible to open any apps. But its best feature is the option to create preset schedules. So let's say you want to focus for two hours starting at three in the afternoon. All you do is preset the periods for the week once, and the app will turn on the focus mode every day for you.

Now, that's a friend!

window and a few tabs to just that subject. By using one window per subject or assignment, you'll find yourself focusing on the single task and less likely to open extra websites to start browsing. When Chrome or Safari is cluttered with hundreds of tabs for each different subject, that's when you find yourself more tempted to wander.

Do you want to take it a step further? Our computers can actually open multiple desktops, allowing us to dedicate one screen per active subject. Your English paper goes on one, history assignment on another, and math help on a third. By zeroing in on one subject per screen or browser window, you're less tempted by outside distractions—and websites—and focus more on what's right in front of you.

Use peer pressure to your advantage. You won't believe how many students work in the library because they feel judged when they veer off from their work and start doing other things on their laptops! Use your computer in a common space but one where you can still get your work done. Whether it's the library, student center, or campus coffeehouse, having other people around will make you less likely to wander from your work.

Plug in the plug-ins. If you seriously feel you lack the self-control to monitor your computer usage, there are dozens of apps and settings that can be installed directly on your computer. These programs allow you to set time periods during which you will have no access to the internet at all or block certain websites from your computer during certain times of the day.

As with any technology, these change daily. However, websites such as Freedom (freedom.to) and the SelfControl app (selfcontrolapp.com) are all great options, providing a variety of ways to block your biggest time robbers.

HOW DO I SOLVE MY DORM ROOM DILEMMA?

"I love studying in my dorm room. My desk is set up perfectly and I have everything I could possibly need right at my fingertips. It puts my mind at ease and makes getting settled in for a long night of review or paper writing less daunting. The only problem? I have a roommate. She's around all the time. When she's in the room she's super noisy and very chatty. It's really distracting. I end up putting off studying if she's already in the room when I get home. I'll walk in and we'll start talking and the next thing I know an hour has gone by and I've gotten nothing done! I get so distracted when she comes in after me that it's hard for me to refocus. I don't know what to do! What are some strategies that I can use to keep myself focused when she is in the room?"

Living with a roommate is tough. Getting used to living in a small shared space definitely takes compromise, trial and error, some sacrifice and lots of planning.

Here are my tried and true tips for cohabitation collaboration:

Stick a whiteboard on the outside door of your room (if your school allows it). The board can be both a place for funny messages and drawings and a great method to politely remind your roommate that you're home and studying. A quick "Hi! I'm in here working!" on the board signals that you'd appreciate some quiet when she opens the door. It also lets her know that while you're OK with a quick hello, it's not time for a blow-by-blow recap of the latest *Bachelor* episode.

A good pair of headphones and a white noise app should be your best friends. They are a must-have on EVERY college student's shopping list. These tools are perfect when you need to drown out noises while working anywhere, but they are especially essential in a dorm room. Plenty of white noise apps can keep you focused while also toning down the sounds of your roommate coming and going or the rest of the residents on your floor playing kickball in the hall.

Desk placement is key! I ask my students to think about **where** they place a desk in their room. Does it face the door? The window? What do you see when you look up? I know it may sound silly or obvious, but **physically** turning your back to distractions can help keep you focused! Put your desk against a blank wall or in the back of your room facing the window. This way, you're less likely to be tempted by hallway noise or what your roommate is doing on their side of the room. It will also send a quiet signal that you are not to be disturbed.

Set up rules for the room. Two people sharing a small space? You need to lay down some serious laws! The dorm has them. Your floor has them. You need them. Discuss everything from who's taking out the garbage to the frequency of overnight guests. Establish a quiet hour—a set time every day where the room is a peaceful oasis that promotes deep work. Trust me, you will thank me for this. Establishing some guidelines when you're not in the heat of the moment is essential to a calm coexistence.

HOW CAN I LIMIT THE TOLL OF THE PHONE SCROLL?

"For my language class, I often have homework assignments in a workbook. I use my phone to listen to music so as not to get distracted by my computer. When I go to change the song (I know I'm not supposed to do that!) or truthfully, by even having it in front of me, I end up distracted by my group texts or social media apps. I end up wasting a lot of time scrolling through them and get completely lost. I've put my phone on 'do not disturb,' but I can still see the notifications when I unlock it. What can I do to make sure I don't get stuck and distracted?"

First, I want to give you props for even taking the steps to try to stay off your computer and put your phone on "do not disturb." That's a great way to start trying to eliminate distractions! But you're right. They're not foolproof. We can find ways to get around them and still end up mindlessly scrolling when we're meant to be working. Procrastination at its best . . . or worst!

Turn off your push notifications. Updating this simple setting for even a few hours every day will eliminate that immediate distraction of the yellow Snapchat ghost or iMessage bubble popping up constantly. If you don't know the notification is there, you're less likely to go searching for it.

Physically bury your messages and social media apps on your phone. I once had a student who had all of her social media apps ungrouped on the first page of her iPhone. This made it incredibly tempting to check all of them **every single time** she unlocked her phone.

Quick fix? Try dragging Instagram, Facebook, Snapchat, and others to the second page and dropping them all in a folder together. The act of having to go in and find them will deter you, and you won't be as tempted by those little red dots. If it takes you more than three steps to do something, you're less likely to do it.

TYPE, TAP, SWIPE, CLICK

Are you in the top 10 percent? Of phone users, that is! A new study by researchers at the app dscout found that the top 10 percent of smartphone users tap or swipe on their phones 5,427 times a day! The rest of us still touch it 2,617 times a day on average. No small number. And according to Gloria Mark, professor at the University of California, Irvine, our average attention span is a mere forty seconds. Can I have your attention?

If this option doesn't work, download your music to listen to off-line and put your phone on airplane mode until your work is completed. Remember that terrific working playlist I mentioned in the homework chapter? Make sure that it is available to listen to off-line. It should be if you're using Apple Music or Spotify. Then turn off Wi-Fi and data for a few hours.

Hide your phone! Or swap with a friend if you're working together. Having one's phone in the same room can reduce that person's cognitive performance. In other words, it makes you stupid. By having our phones out, we have to work twice as hard to resist the temptation to use them. But when we hide them or swap with a friend, that enticement disappears. Try zipping it into a pocket inside your backpack if you're in the library, or sticking it under your pillow or in the closet if you're in your room. Close enough to connect to your Bluetooth headphones but nowhere you'll be tempted to check it.

Physically take yourself off the grid. Put your phone on airplane mode or subscribe to the notion of "out of sight, out of mind." If there's no way to reach you or for you to check social media, you eliminate the distractions and put the focus back on your work.

Classroom Confessionals
What's something you do to study that none of your friends do?
"I watch television to get through the grunt work." —Matt, college junior

DO YOU HAVE FOMO?

FOMO is the fear of missing out—on something more interesting, more exciting or just plain better than what you're currently doing. To counteract that nagging pit in your stomach, you constantly stay connected with others, so you don't miss something important or exciting.

Or, as I like to describe it, you're watching your social life fly by on social media or through your text messages 24-7 while experiencing heart-wrenching dread that you'll miss out on something that will threaten your social status. How did I do?

How do you know if you have FOMO? Ask yourself the following questions:

Is your phone never more than six inches away?

Do you keep your phone next to you during meals? While watching television? When you're sitting on the toilet?

Are you texting friends or checking your social media accounts during class time or at school?

When studying or doing homework, can you go longer than six minutes before giving in to the urge to check your phone?

Is your phone the first thing you reach for the minute you wake up? When you go to sleep?

The point of this exercise is not for me to tell you you're spending too much time on your phone. It's not even to tell you how much is appropriate. The point is for YOU to truly figure out if your technology use is seriously affecting your well-being, your academic performance and, yes, your ability to get stuff done. I know, it always comes back to that. But if that is the case, then devising serious strategies to manage your time on your devices is the point. Grab ideas from this chapter or seek help from a parent or friend to put a plan in place. The bottom line? Only YOU really know how much is too much. So it's time to get real.

❓ HOW CAN I FEND OFF THE INTERRUPTER?

"I love working in the library. I feel like I'm not working alone, yet having everyone working around me forces me to get my work done too. It's the perfect mix of social and quiet. The problem? I have this one friend who, even if I'm clearly working on a different subject, constantly interrupts me with questions about the class we take together. It's so frustrating. I do my best to answer, but it takes me so long to get myself back into 'other-class mode.' What's the best way for me to refocus without having to give up my favorite work spot?"

I hear this a lot. The mix of quiet and social can be the perfect recipe for getting shit done. But getting back into the groove after being interrupted for any reason, especially one that requires you to switch your brain to an entirely different subject and then back again, can be distracting. When you're working on something and turn away, it takes your brain a full twenty minutes to refocus. The constant switching back and forth, or even the tiniest of interruptions, can lose you valuable studying time and—understandably—lead to frustration.

So how do we politely tell them they need to stop and refocus when they don't listen and inevitably do it anyway?

Counteroffer. Working with someone on a subject can actually be really helpful to reinforce what you already know and get help with what you don't. So don't be so quick to dismiss your friend outright! However, you don't need to do so on your friend's clock and calendar. Counteroffer! Saying something like "I really need to finish my calc homework first, but in an hour, I'll be available to discuss history" could benefit you.

X marks the spot. When you read a book and need to stop, don't you always bookmark your page? This makes picking up where you left off a breeze. Apply the same technique when you get interrupted. Take out a piece of paper or a sticky note and jot down exactly what you were working on. Even include what you were thinking about or what you were going to do next. This technique will allow you to easily get back into gear and regain your focus.

Lean into the interruptions. The likelihood that this works all the time is, unfortunately, slim. So, how can you quickly refocus yourself while still making the most of these interruptions? The quickest—and most obvious—answer is to say, "not right now" and continue, but how about leaning into the interruption and taking a break? I know this tip goes against some of my previous advice, but sometimes the effort to do something else takes more time than just doing what is presented in front of us. Take this opportunity to work with your friend. Viewing the interruption as an unplanned break or needed work session will reduce frustrations and have you getting back to your other work with a better mind-set.

PUT IT TO THE TEST . . . THE BATTERY TEST

Here's a fun game to play. Want to see how much time you actually spend on your phone? Specifically, all your texting, social media, game playing, even shopping? Grab your phone (iPhone only) and go to Settings. From there, go to Battery. Scroll down to Battery Health. Here you can choose "Last 24 Hours" or "Last 10 Days." Pick "Last 24 Hours" and scroll a bit more. BINGO! Your usage by percentages. You can't argue with the data! Eye-opening, I'm sure!

HOW CAN I AVOID THE VIDEO GAME VORTEX?

"I'm super busy almost every day after school and rarely have time to hang out with my friends. When I get home from my after-school activities, my friends are usually playing video games together and want me to log on. It's a constant stream of friends who are always online, so I get sucked in and can never pull myself away to do my homework. I find myself with too little time to get my homework done. This causes a ton of stress between me and my parents. What can I do to socialize with my friends over video games, but make sure I'm leaving enough time to get my studying and responsibilities around the house done?"

Video games are a time suck. And they are a really easy way to lose track of time and procrastinate. It makes sense! Games these days are never-ending, and the social aspect of being able to talk to and play with your friends can make it feel as if you're all together, which makes it harder to disconnect. I'm all for the need to unwind after school activities. I advocate for it. But not when it's stopping you from doing what needs to get done!

Set up a blackout hour. You might want to involve your parents in this one, because a *blackout hour* translates to no phones, no TV and no screens—for everyone in your home. And while it's usually met with a bit of protest, my families learn to love it.

Being forced to shut down for an hour or so every night allows you the uninterrupted and nonnegotiable time to finish assignments, prepare for the next day and reset. And the best part? When your friends ask why you have to log off a video chat or turn off the video

Classroom Confessionals
Biggest distraction while studying and how do you handle it?
"My phone. I put it in my backpack so I can't see or touch it."
—Alex, college junior

games, you can easily blame it on your parents! Saving face and getting work done sounds like a pretty good deal to me!

All kidding aside, a blackout hour is a really effective way to refocus your attention away from video games and help you budget your screen time appropriately.

Track your gaming time. Create a gaming log—either a spreadsheet or just a piece of paper. Write down the time you start playing a game, which game and when you stop. Total up your gaming time at the end of each week. Seeing that huge number just might snap you out of your video vortex!

? HOW CAN I WORK THROUGH THE SOUND OF SILENCE?

"More days than not I come home after school to an empty house. While this should be the perfect environment for me to sit down and get my homework done, it's almost *too* quiet and I find myself distracted by what's around me or getting up to get a snack, pet my dog, or walk around the house, with no one there to refocus me and get me back to work. I've tried working both in my room at my desk and at the dining room table, but nothing seems to get the job 100 percent done. How do I get started without a push?"

Tack up the to-dos. Is someone around to leave you a list of things you have to get done? Coming home to explicit instructions may be enough to replicate the feeling of having someone to guide you toward your to-dos. And you'll feel as if you're on a deadline. Knowing you need to have a few tasks checked off by the time someone gets home is a great motivator!

Cue the music. Working alone at home means music without headphones! Put on some background noise, crank up your playlist, or blast tunes from the stereo! As you learned in the homework chapter, music can mimic the presence of other people.

Connect virtually. This is my favorite tip, and I do this ALL the time with my students. It's called Body Doubling! If you need someone to help you get unstuck and started, beam up a friend virtually. You work on your end. They work on theirs. No talking. No chatting. Just someone on the other side, keeping you focused and on task. No friend to call? You can easily schedule an appointment with an accountability coach by using the app Focusmate.

Pull out your Personal Homework Profile. That's what it's there for. Having your best practices in place will provide you that road map you need when none other exists.

> **Classroom Confessionals**
> **What's the largest assignment you've completed in the shortest amount of time?**
> "Ten-page paper in one night."
> —Jared, college junior

Chapter 8
"I'M NOT IN THE MOOD"

MOTIVATION

"I'm not in the mood to study right now. I'm going to have a snack first and then start."
"I'm going to get going on my homework after I check Instagram."
"Just one more YouTube video! Then I'll take out the trash. Promise!"

I hear these excuses constantly, whether you have an exam to study for, homework due the next day or even a quick chore around the house. I get it. It's tough to always be in the right frame of mind at the right time of day to do what is basically . . . the right thing! But I know and you know that eventually you need to get in the mood to get done what you don't want to do.

And some of you believe that "if I do one thing first that makes me really, really happy, I'll be in a better mood and then I'll be able to get going on those things that don't make me happy."

So you want the good news? What you're feeling has validity.

A lot of research conducted in the last few years shows that some types of procrastination are mood-based. (This is actually really cool research, so listen up!)

Timothy Pychyl, an associate professor of psychology at Carleton University in Ottawa, Canada, and head of their Procrastination Research Group, explains that procrastinators often attempt to avoid the anxiety, fear or boredom brought on by a tough task with activities aimed at "repairing their mood" or, as he refers to this pattern, "giving in to feeling good." We assume we need to do something that will put us in a good or better mood, such as checking social media or watching a favorite television show, before we can tackle what we're putting off.

Guilty as charged.

Now the bad news. No, you won't feel like doing it later. When you put something off and tell yourself you'll do it later, you feel good at that moment. "Yay! I don't have to do the damn thing right now!" But when later comes, you still don't feel like doing it. And this pattern makes you feel worse when you realize how much time you've wasted or you never accomplished what you intended to.

So what does this theory look like in your life?

YOUR STORY

Let's say you come home from school and have that pesky English paper on *Jane Eyre* to write. You're dreading it. The book was boring. You despise the class. You hate to write. You're tired. You're just not in the mood. Instead of sitting down and getting to work, you say, "I'm going to do something that will put me in a better mood first before I can deal with this miserable paper."

So you turn on Netflix and promise yourself that you'll only watch one episode. And after that episode, you'll feel better and get going. But before you know it, three hours have gone by and you're on your fourth episode.

Is your mood any better? Maybe. But that good feeling will be super short-lived. Soon you will likely feel worse than you did when you first walked in the door. Maybe because you've wasted a ton of time. Maybe because the paper is due tomorrow and you won't be able to hand it in on time. Maybe now that you have fewer hours to work on it, you think you're going to do a pretty crappy job. Or you're staring down the possible wrath of your teacher or parents.

So how do we break this cycle and get you motivated? Truthfully, this is a tricky one. Because not all reasons for a lack of motivation are obvious or an easy fix. No time management skills? A learned skill. Lack of study tools? There are loads of them for you to pick from.

But what if your lack of "being in the mood" goes deeper? Perhaps you have perfectionist tendencies. Or you simply don't like what you need to do. Maybe you're not confident in your abilities and fear doing poorly. Or you think you're lazy. And possibly you're confused or overwhelmed about getting started.

We're all wired to put things off for different reasons, but we also have the capacity to overcome them.

There's a reason I opted to have this chapter as the book's last. All the tips and tools, all the suggestions and strategies, everything

TIME TRAVEL

One of my favorite exercises to do with my students when that procrastination plague is at an all-time high is time traveling. Imagine this scenario: You're trying to psych yourself up to study for midterms when all you really want to do is scour Reddit. How do you make sure you do the right thing? Project yourself into the future, after you've completed your work, and imagine how good you're going to feel. I like to do it on a rating scale of one to ten.

"How good will you feel in two hours when you've written four pages of your paper?"

Or you can try the reverse. "How poorly will you feel after two hours that you haven't gotten anything done?" Really allow yourself to experience these positive and negative feelings in your imagination. Put yourself in a feel-good scenario, such as being able to spend time with friends later on, or in a consequence-based one of working late into the night, so that you can really change your procrastination patterns.

we've covered in the previous chapters can help you override some of these behaviors and hopefully help you figure out what might be truly getting in your way.

So let's dive into some of the more common emotional reasons why you might feel unmotivated and go over some essential strategies to help you put those tendencies to rest. (Alert! There are a few repeats from previous chapters.)

DOES FEAR OF DOING POORLY OR FAILING KEEP YOU FROM MOBILIZING?

How many times has the fear of *what might happen* prevented you from taking action on something you need to do or should be doing? The result? Up went your guard and out poured the excuses.

"I did a really crappy job on this project, so I'd rather not turn it in than turn it in and get a really bad grade."

"I'm afraid to email my professor and ask for an extension on my paper. What if he gets angry?"

"I don't want to apply for that job because I know other kids are more qualified than me and I'm afraid of getting rejected."

"I've already fallen so far behind in my reading and I'll never catch up. Why bother?"

Fear is messy and uncomfortable, and it makes us feel like crap. So our usual go-to is to avoid things we're afraid of at all costs. BUT we also know that the buildup or anticipation of something we fear is usually way worse than the fear that results from the task or situation itself, and that we pay a lot more in consequences for a head-in-the-sand stance. The good news is that knowing that is half the battle, because if you know that you're powerless to prevent feeling fearful, then YOU can also be intentional about changing your relationship to it.

It's time to get real and face your fears. As best-selling author Tim Ferriss explains in his powerful TED Talk (Google it!), we are better off *fear setting*, or visualizing all the bad things that could happen to us, so we become less afraid of taking action. This strategy helps us overcome self-paralysis and spurs action, because what we fear most or find uncomfortable is exactly what we actually need to be doing. He encourages clearly defining both costs and benefits of our fears to lessen their power.

So the next time you find yourself unmotivated and fearful of the "what if?" ask yourself the following questions:

"How bad will this really be?"

"What's the worst thing that can happen?"

"And if the worst thing happens, what can I do to lessen the severity?"

And my favorite, *"What's worse? Doing something that's hard or that I'm afraid of? Or not doing it at all?"* Where will YOU pay the biggest consequence?

An honest answer just might fuel a positive breakthrough.

IS GETTING STARTED OVERWHELMING?

Are you spinning in circles? So overwhelmed that starting something has you doing anything but? Here are some of my suggestions:

Make getting started simple. Begin with something so easy and so small that success is literally guaranteed. One sentence to write. One math problem to solve. One page to read. You get the idea. Chances are that once you get started, you'll keep on going. The dread that drives procrastination is almost always exaggerated. So when you see that you can do the task or assignment you were avoiding, you'll usually gain the confidence to keep going.

Break it down. Way down. I can't stress this enough. We know that breaking things down into manageable parts makes working through them less overwhelming. It also provides multiple

WHAT'S YOUR MVP?

Some say that perfection is the enemy of completion. I agree. But it is also the enemy of getting started! We tend to feel we need to put out our very best work the first time out of the gate. Every Single Time. Being stuck on writing a perfectly thought-out and organized paper the first time you sit down to work on it can prevent you from getting started. Here's where your MVP comes in. An MVP is your *minimum viable product*, a term used in product development, in which you build your product with the least number of bells and whistles first, to get feedback for future product development later.

And with that feedback, you THEN build up!

So what does an MVP look like? A few bullet points showcasing your ideas for your business class project to show your professor. Your outline for your AP government paper. Or the first chapter of your new book to show your editors to make sure you're on the right track. If you look at your MVP as a way to get the necessary feedback and validation to improve on your initial work, it will save you time in the long run and help you get unstuck and started. Brilliant!

opportunities for smaller successes. And with success comes the acknowledgment to stay motivated. So instead of putting "write paper" on your homework to-do list, try writing, "find five sources," "craft outline," "begin opening paragraph." It's much easier to accomplish each one of these steps, which makes it easier for you to initiate and finish!

Get your GPS on. You need to figure out where you're going before you get started. I'm talking about creating a road map to help you find your way. Write it down. Get it out of your head and onto paper where YOU CAN SEE IT. Research shows that if you WRITE it, you are more likely to commit to DOING it. It holds you accountable and makes it real.

Separate the setup from the task. If you make setting up for the task a task of its own and only focus on getting that done, it will make getting started easier. So what does that look like? Say you want to study for your economics midterm. Focus first on collecting your notes and old homework. Gather any study guides or tools you have previously prepared. Figure out what study methods you are going to use to prepare for this exam. Merely starting gives us a small sense of accomplishment and the confidence to keep going.

DO YOU THINK YOU'RE LAZY?

I hate this word. How can such a small word carry so much weight? It produces shame. Guilt. Competitiveness. We live in a culture that awards busyness and frowns on idleness. Busyness has become a badge of honor. Being busy must mean you are being more productive.

SO NOT TRUE.

Let's chat about what laziness isn't. Lazy isn't curling up on a comfortable chair and reading. Lazy isn't taking a nap. Lazy isn't going for a walk to clear your head. Nor is it just *being*.

I also don't believe anyone is truly lazy. That doesn't mean we don't all have a few lazy moments sometimes. However, I think there is always some conscious thought and self-perception going on underneath the surface that produces that feeling of laziness. We're tough on ourselves.

Some say laziness is an absence of action. But I don't agree. I feel laziness is an action, as you are making a choice to do one thing (or nothing) vs another. A wise man once told me that making a decision to NOT do something is still making a decision. And, therefore, you are taking action.

Laziness is good for the body and mind . . . when done right. We need time to repair and renew. To put gas back in the tank. To sit with our thoughts.

The perception of laziness truly resonates with me. For the longest time I felt that if I wasn't in constant motion, that I would be perceived as lazy, unproductive, even unworthy. But keeping up that pace completely depleted me. It was essential for my well-being and my productiveness to give myself permission to schedule my lazy time. Or as I like to call it: **scheduling the unscheduled**. And I encourage my students to do the same. Here's Ethan's story.

ETHAN'S STORY

Ethan was pretty beaten down when we first met. A second-semester college freshman, he was on academic probation, having failed two classes the previous semester. As we dug into the details, his self-proclaimed laziness and procrastination were a constant throughout our conversations, even though he had juggled eighteen credits, a part-time job, visiting his ill father and countless other responsibilities. He equated being lazy with procrastinating. So I asked him to share his schedule with me, specifically how he juggled all he had on his plate and where he felt he had "slacked off." His term, not mine.

Ethan started school at ninety miles an hour and his speed never let up. With no structure or routine in place or any downtime in his schedule, he worked whenever he could find the time—between classes, early in the morning before work, during meals and when visiting with his dad. Since he felt that he had to activate all the time, he burned out quickly and began avoiding his work at all costs.

I worked with Ethan to add unscheduled time to his schedule each week. He gave himself permission to take Saturdays completely off. To do whatever he wanted on that one day. Sleep until noon and play video games? He had that option. If he wanted to visit his dad, he did. And if he chose to get ahead in his classes, he could do that too. This scheduling of the unscheduled completely changed Ethan's mind-set and productivity. Since Saturday was his to do whatever he desired, he had no problem activating and staying motivated on Sundays or burning the late-night candle during the week. Unscheduled Saturdays, as he called them, were his much-needed mind break.

DO YOU HATE WHAT YOU HAVE TO DO?

Let's face it. Sometimes we just have to do what we don't like. Here are my two favorite tricks when I'm faced with a dreaded task:

Pair something you love with something you don't. There is a reason why I do laundry Monday nights while I watch the *Bachelor*. I hate folding laundry and find it much easier while indulging in my favorite reality television program. Remember my student Sam and his beloved popcorn? Pairing something you love with something you don't just makes that pill so much easier to swallow! What tasks that you dislike can you pair with ones you enjoy doing?

Reward yourself. Don't underestimate the power of an anticipated reward. Frozen yogurt. An episode of the *Bachelor*. Poking around on Nordstrom.com. (OK, that's my list.) Build in rewards! When you complete something that you truly don't want to be doing, that merits celebrating. Like marching-band-worthy celebrating! You've earned it.

ARE YOU CONFUSED?

Get clear expectations. Nothing will kill your motivation more than if you don't have a clear idea of what needs to be done and the steps needed to get there. So whether it's working on your science project or cleaning up the backyard, you will be able to activate if the expectations, instructions and timelines of the task are specific. To the extent that you can, get clarity on your tasks and what it will take to complete them. This will truly help you eliminate the confusion, perform optimally and ultimately stop procrastinating. And build some self-activating skills in the process.

> **Classroom Confessionals**
> **What's something you do to study that none of your friends do?**
> "Study out loud!" —Cole, college junior

IT'S ALL IN THE SYLLABUS!

The syllabus? The thing I skim over on the first day of class and rarely look at again? Yes! For students who are true perfectionist procrastinators, I find that using the information given in their syllabi that shows how much specific assignments are worth is perfectionism gold! How so? When they see the different percentages assigned to various class expectations, it helps them prioritize their assignments, which helps them determine how much time they need to spend on each. So, for example, if a homework assignment is worth only 5 percent of their grade, but their midterm is worth 40 percent, they know that spending time making each homework assignment perfect won't move the grade needle much, but digging in to study for the midterm will. This works especially well when they have several assignments due at the same time in different classes. Are you going to spend more time on your psychology paper that is worth 50 percent of your grade or an astronomy lab worth 10 percent?

DOES IT HAVE TO BE PERFECT?

Let's get a few things straight. No one is perfect all the time. Can we just get that out of the way?

Not your friend posting the perfectly crafted Instagram picture. Not your physics classmate who seems to know the correct answer to every question asked. No one.

Sometimes striving for perfection is a good thing. Some of you may use your perfectionism to stay motivated. Others work to achieve goals and strive for achievements that require extraordinary effort, skill and detail. Your perfectionism is synonymous with being driven. And you certainly know how to keep your eyes on the road. There's nothing wrong with that.

However, can we also agree that perfectionism can derail you? It can make you stuck. Set you up for unrealistic expectations and standards that are impossible to achieve. Make it impossible for you to make a mistake and, therefore, not have an opportunity to learn from it. Or do I dare say . . . cause you to procrastinate?

I've heard all the perfectionist comments there are.

"If I can't do it perfectly, then why do it at all?"

"I can't get this paper to be perfect, so I'd rather quit."

"My parents expect perfect grades and that's impossible for me. So I won't even try."

"What will people say if my performance is not perfect? It's easier if I just don't audition."

Any sound familiar?

Here are a few strategies to help:

Get comfortable with making mistakes. Work on trying to change your mind-set. Not easy, I know. Refer back to the fear-setting exercise earlier to help you through. And remember, no one will remember you made a mistake. They'll remember how you handled it.

The Digital Download
Forest

Is there anything more motivating than an app that also helps the environment? Forest's simple mission is to help users be present and stay focused. To put down their phones! When you spend time away from your phone, you grow virtual trees and earn coins, which can be saved up and used to help plant REAL trees. Forest partners with Trees for the Future to help plant real trees throughout the world. What a feel-good!

Work with a deadline in mind. Real or fake. It doesn't matter. If your tendency is to keep editing, keep tweaking and keep studying, then setting a date or time to finish and move on is critical. This is where your timer or calendar are extremely useful!

You need to create a structure that forces you to curb that tunnel vision. Repeat after me: it's good enough.

If your perfectionism is keeping you from starting, call in the troops. Tell a friend you want to have the first draft of your paper completed by Wednesday or your audition monologue memorized by Saturday. Ask them to hold you accountable. Knowing you have a check-in date or time for completion is a sure way to get started.

Forgive yourself. We get super angry with ourselves when we procrastinate over and over. Research shows that all that negativity is making the problem worse. We need to be kind to ourselves or forgive ourselves for our procrastination, so we focus on trying again instead of beating ourselves up about it. That's a strategy I can get behind!

**I want to be careful here with my advice. If your perfectionism is truly getting in the way of your health and well-being, please talk to your parents, counselor or coach. They can offer guidance and support.

TEN QUESTIONS TO OVERCOME PROCRASTINATION PUSHBACK

Below is a series of questions I've developed over the years that my students use again and again whenever they're stuck in their procrastination cycle. I have found that asking yourself questions, specifically the right questions, can help change your mind-set, stretch your thinking and help you uncover the answers you need to get unstuck and started.

I'm hoping that whenever you feel the need for support, you'll refer back to this list as well.

1. **What is my plan . . .** after dinner, this weekend, to study for my math quiz when I get home from soccer so late, have to wake up early for Spanish club or (fill in the blank)?
   Asking this question in this manner helps you to develop a sense of time. Some of you have a very difficult time making the connection that what you have to do later in the day or even later in the week or month can affect what needs to be done now. This question is an organic way for you to begin to formulate routines and schedules and remember what you need to accomplish.

2. **What do I need to do to . . .** get ready for soccer, get ready for school, take out the trash or whatever else?
   Formulating the answer to this question helps you build a mental checklist for what needs to be done and how to do it. That checklist helps you build your memory. And when you build memory, you build habits and routines. You start to remember!

3. **What is the first step for . . .** starting my science project, studying for my test, writing my college essay or (fill in the blank)?
   Are you easily overwhelmed? Does trying to visualize a whole project

all at once leave you not knowing where to start? This question will bring your focus to a manageable starting point and help you begin.

4. **What am I going to do before, after, in an hour, after dinner, after rehearsal?**
Using concrete language helps you visualize what comes next, reinforcing your time sense.

5. **What are my priorities today?** With regard to getting homework done, for instance.
Defining your priorities instead of listing your to-dos requires your brain to do some significant heavy lifting to determine order, sequence and importance.

6. **What could get in my way today (or tonight or this weekend) that would interfere with my getting my homework (or chores) done?**
Asking what could get in your way allows you to see the whole picture—extracurricular activities, social plans or even dinner with Grandma—so you can plan accordingly.

7. **What is the smallest thing I'm willing to do?**
Eliminating barriers to entry helps get you into gear.

8. **What does "done" look like?** followed by . . . **What do I need to do to get to done? What materials do I need? How much time?**
I love these questions! Why? Because if you have a hard time initiating, looking at the end and working backward creates a road map for you to follow.

9. **How am I going to remember to remember?**
Are you going to write it down? Take a photo? Text it to yourself? The list is endless.

10. **And . . . what DO I know?**
Anytime you start to say, "I don't know" in response to a question, asking "What do I know?" helps you see where the breakdown—the difference between the known and the unknown—is. And seeing the breakdown often reveals a natural answer or solution.

BEFORE YOU GO

YOU DID IT! You made it to the end! The first step in managing your procrastination!

I often get asked if every one of my students is a success story. Are they able to make permanent changes in their daily lives that last?

No. But most of them are. And here are the three significant lessons that had the most impact in turning their habits and mind-set around.

1. **To truly manage your procrastination, you need a plan each and every day.** Consistent planning requires figuring out what works for you, and more importantly, what doesn't. Anyone can try a quick fix. But I hope that after reading this book you are able to identify the tools and techniques or systems and strategies that truly spoke to you so that you can tap into them regularly to keep you motivated and on track.

2. **Procrastination-busting skills are learned skills.** To master them, you must practice them. They're not one-and-done skills—that is, skills to be learned once and moved on from. That could not be further from the truth. There is no magic elixir here. Consistency is key.

3. **Incorporating just one small positive change will lead to making more.** And permanent changes take time. So don't get discouraged. Trust yourself. Keep working at it and try different approaches until you find what works.

I've designed this book to be a valuable resource you can refer to again and again, and hopefully find something new and useful each time you do. No matter what, give yourself credit for your accomplishments.

This is just the beginning. I'm thrilled to be part of your journey.

COULD IT BE SOMETHING ELSE?

If you sense that you are procrastinating more than others your age or your chronic procrastination is severely affecting your life, it's worth considering that something else may be going on. I encourage you to discuss your concerns with your parents or caregivers, a teacher you feel close to, your school counselor or therapist or the counseling services department at your college.

Please don't wait. Remember, you are your best advocate and know when something doesn't feel quite right. Reach out to get help. There are people in your life who can help you.

ACKNOWLEDGMENTS

When you tell your family and friends that you're going to write another book and in record time and during your business's busiest season, you're met with many headshakes and eye rolls. But you put your head down and work to make it happen. Because you know that there's a community of people surrounding you who will support you. No matter what you do.

Much gratitude to the team at Lerner Publishing and especially Hallie Warshaw, book developer extraordinaire, for your professional support and collaboration throughout the process. And thank you to Julie Bestry for introducing us!

Thanks to my terrific husband, Wayne, who always keeps a straight face when I tell him the next crazy idea I'm about to take on. No questions asked. His quiet belief in me knows no bounds.

And thanks to my loves, Maddie and Eli, who acted as my sounding board, think tank, focus group and toughest editors. Your contributions are immeasurable.

To the smartest, loveliest and hardest-working women I know, the Order Out of Chaos Team. You kept it all together when I was falling apart. You showed nothing but grace and commitment during the insanity. I'm so lucky to work alongside you.

I'd like to express appreciation to my professional community, the National Association of Productivity and Organizing Professionals, who have taught me so much about what it means to truly "give to get" and a special shout-out to the RCG for your cheerleading and mentorship.

And to my fabulous friends. You know who you are! Thank you for all the check-ins, phone calls and words of encouragement. How lucky can a girl be?

And a very special thank-you to all my students and their families who have let me into their lives over the last sixteen years. I don't take that privilege lightly. It's been an honor to help you.

RESOURCES

So many resources are available that it's impossible to list them all. I have rounded up my favorite websites, books, products and apps that I recommend to my students to help them manage their procrastination, learn time management and study skills, get organized and stay on track.

Visit howtodoitnowbook.com for downloadable copies of the forms and charts throughout this book.

BOOKS

Guare, Richard, Peg Dawson, and Colin Guare. *Smart but Scattered Teens: The "Executive Skills" Program for Helping Teens Reach Their Potential.* New York: Guilford, 2013.

Homayoun, Ana. *That Crumpled Paper Was Due Last Week: Helping Disorganized and Distracted Boys Succeed in School and Life.* New York: Perigee, 2010.

Josel, Leslie. *What's the Deal with Teens and Time Management: A Parents' Guide to Helping Your Teen Succeed.* Pennington, NJ: People Tested Books, 2015.

Kulman, Randy. *Train Your Brain for Success: A Teenager's Guide to Executive Functions.* Plantation, FL: Specialty Press, 2012.

WEBSITES

audible.com

khanacademy.org

koofers.com

lifehacker.com

orderoochaos.com

ratemyprofessors.com

ALARMS, CLOCKS AND TIMERS

Analog clocks: available at Amazon or other stores

Clocky: clocky.com

Focus Booster: focusboosterapp.com

Focus Time: focustimeapp.com

Time Timer: timetimer.com

Wake N Shake Alarm Clock App: apps.apple.com

WatchMinder: watchminder.com

DIGITAL FILE MANAGEMENT

Evernote: evernote.com

Dropbox: dropbox.com

ELECTRONIC CALENDARS

Google Calendar: play.google.com/store

Microsoft Outlook Calendar: support.office.com

HOMEWORK HELPERS

Brainly: brainly.com

MyHomework Student Planner App: myhomeworkapp.com

Purdue Online Writing Lab: owl.purdue.edu/owl/purdue_owl.html

SparkNotes: sparknotes.com

MEDIA DISTRACTION APPS

Freedom: freedom.to

Cold Turkey: getcoldturkey.com

Offtime App: play.google.com/store

SelfControl: selfcontrolapp.com

StayFocused: stayfocused.com

PAPER: LONG-TERM STORAGE

Open-top file box: Available at Amazon or office supply stores

Smead expanding file jackets: smead.com

PAPER: SHORT-TERM STORAGE

Avery Big Tab Insertable Two-Pocket Plastic Dividers: avery.com

Case-it binders: caseit.com/home

C-Line Binder Pockets with Write-on Index Tabs: c-lineproducts.com

Letter-sized sheet protectors: Target or office supply stores

Like-It magazine holders: containerstore.com

Samsill DUO 2-in-1 Organizer: samsill.com

Wilson Jones Big Mouth Filers: wilsonjones.com

PLANNERS AND CALENDARS

Order Out of Chaos Academic Planner: A Tool for Time Management: products.orderoochaos.com

Planner Pads: plannerpads.com

Post-it Notes Weekly Calendar: post-it.com

PRODUCTIVITY TOOLS

Coach.me: www.coach.me

Focusmate: focusmate.com

The Habit Hub: thehabithub.com

StickK: stickk.com

Todoist: todoist.com

SCHOOL SUPPLIES

Crazy Aaron's Thinking Putty: puttyworld.com

Graphic organizers: superteacherworksheets.com

Grid-It organizer: cocooninnovations.com

Pencil pouch with mesh window: Available at office supply stores

Post-It Super Sticky Big Notes: post-it.com

SimpleMind: simplemind.eu

Wide-ruled reinforced notebook paper: Available at office supply stores

SEATING

Balance ball chairs: gaiam.com

Bungee office chairs: containerstore.com

STREAMING MUSIC SERVICES

Apple Music: apple.com/music

Brain.fm: brain.fm

Spotify: spotify.com

STUDY SKILLS/DIGITAL TOOLS

Khan Academy: khanacademy.org

Quizlet: quizlet.com

StudyBlue: studyblue.com

STUDY SKILLS/NOTE-TAKING

Dragon Speech Recognition: nuance.com/dragon

Livescribe: livescribe.com

STUDY SPACE AND DESKS

Lap desk: Available at Amazon or office supply stores

Privacy shields: reallygoodstuff.com

Sit to stand desks: Available at Amazon or office supply stores

Three-sided presentation board: Available at office supply stores

INDEX

ABOUT THE AUTHOR

Leslie Josel, an academic/life coach for teens and college students, is an award-winning entrepreneur who founded Order Out of Chaos—an organization inspired by her efforts to help her son after he was diagnosed with ADHD—to help students learn the necessary skills to experience success in learning and in life.

She is also an award-winning author, creator of an academic planner that helps students master time management skills, and an internationally acclaimed speaker on topics spanning from time management to raising problem solvers to procrastination.

Leslie continues to learn from her son and her audiences, sharing her observations with readers of *ADDitude* magazine in her weekly column, Dear ADHD Family Coach. She has also written for other print and digital magazines such as *Family Circle*, *Diabetes Self-Management* and Lifehacker.com.

In 2018 Leslie was awarded the National Association of Productivity & Organizing Professionals' (NAPO's) Founders' Award, given in the spirit of the original five founders of NAPO and presented to a member whose outstanding contributions have helped advance the organizing and productivity profession. Global Gurus also named her one of the top ten time management experts in the world four years in a row.

Leslie lives in Larchmont, New York, with her husband, Wayne. Her son, Eli, is a recent graduate of Ithaca College and her daughter, Madelyn, lives and works in New York City. In her all-too-rare spare time, Leslie can be found hiding out in her car, indulging in her favorite treats—frozen yogurt and entertainment magazines.

To sign up for the Order Out of Chaos monthly newsletter, read their weekly blog, access free videos, resources and information or learn more about products and services, visit their website at orderoochaos.com.

You can also find Leslie on social media:

Twitter: @orderoochaos
Facebook: orderoutofchaos
Instagram: order.out.of.chaos

Pinterest: Order Out of Chaos
YouTube: Leslie Josel